COLETTE

Elaine Marks

COLETTE

Rutgers University Press
New Brunswick, New Jersey

Copyright © 1960 by Rutgers, The State University
Library of Congress Catalogue Card Number: 60–9694
Manufactured in the United States of America by H. Wolff
Designed by Marshall Lee

to my parents

The existence of this book is due in large part to the invaluable criticisms and encouragements of Professor Germaine Brée of New York University and to the skilful editorial assistance of Edith Warren. I am also grateful to the United States Government Fulbright Program which allowed me to spend a year in Paris doing research on Colette. Finally I should like to give special thanks to Monsieur Maurice Goudeket who, in permitting me to work in Colette's Palais Royal apartment on certain of her manuscripts, made it possible for me to come a little closer both to the woman and to her work.

Elaine Marks

Contents

COLETTE

I

Why Colette?

"Regarde"

Sidonie Gabrielle Colette died on the third of August, 1954. An enigmatic and capricious young girl, a vigorous and ubiquitous woman, a suffering yet stolid octogenarian, her name had passed into the annals of French literary and social history long before her death. "Notre Grande Colette," "Chère Colette," "Madame Colette"—these varied appellations refer to and recall some of the visages or masks which Colette, at different periods of her career and her life, seemed to have assumed: a feminine Colette, a masculine Colette, a bourgeois Colette, a Bohemian Colette, a stoical Colette, Colette the great lady of French letters.

Lying on her couch, which looked over the arcades and trees of the Palais Royal, Colette had for many years received the praise and affection of both her illustrious and her unknown countrymen. At her death they came in impressive numbers to stand before the coffin placed in the garden of the Palais Royal, to hear the official speeches (for Colette had been refused burial by the Catholic Church [1] and was given instead a state burial by representatives of the French Fourth Republic) and to mourn a name, a face, a legend. . . .

During her lifetime Colette had received and accepted as much official recognition as any other French writer of the first half of the twentieth century. She was a member of the Royal Belgian Academy of Letters, a member and president of the Goncourt Academy, and in 1953 she was made *Grand Officier* of the Legion of Honor. Her writings were placed in school texts and anthologies alongside such consecrated authors as Chateaubriand and Rousseau. On her eightieth birthday one of the leading French literary weeklies, *Le Figaro Littéraire*, with the aid of many prominent French writers and critics, had paid homage to her life and work. At the time of her death almost every important French newspaper devoted space to lament the passing of a woman who had for so many years seemed a permanent fixture of French life, a national institution.

In France, the demise of a prominent author is often a public event and always a literary one. It is the time to praise or to damn, to write recollections of the deceased, to search for letters and unpublished writings. This is, for the dead writer, a most crucial period. Colette emerged from the ritual post-mortems essentially unscathed, but nonetheless somewhat mistreated. Because she had become virtually sacrosanct and because her writings seemed unrelated to the contemporary mood, little attempt was made to redefine or even to reread Colette's work. What was said after her death, both by her admirers and her detractors, was a repetition of what had been said for almost twenty-five years, a reiteration of clichés. Colette was in danger of becoming immortal and unknown.

She has been called the first prose writer of her age, the great stylist, the creator of novels "prehistoric" [2] in their subject matter and lacking in moral and metaphysical dimensions,[3] the author who "eludes analysis." [4] And all these comments are partially valid. In general, Colette's novels deal with a strictly marginal social group, the demimonde or borderline demimonde of the turn of the century. There is a moral dimension in Colette's work, but it is not, and with good reason, glaringly apparent. Colette is essentially a psychologist of the senses, a poet of the sensuous. She transmits the world as it is, not as it might or should be. Perhaps because of this, because the critic feels that there is so little for him to hold on to, Colette's work seems to "elude analysis."

The real difficulty is that it is impossible to treat Colette merely as a novelist. She is the author of short stories, anecdotes, plays, dramatic criticism, chronicles, prefaces, personal reminiscences and meditations, portraits of men, animals and flowers. Of the forty or more separate works written by Colette, only eighteen may properly be termed novels. Although several of these novels can and indeed do stand by themselves as works of some stature, understanding and appreciation both of them and of Colette as a writer are enhanced by a study of the relationships between her fiction and nonfiction, between the diversity and unity of her world.

As Colette's life was often obscured by her work, so her work was often obscured by her life, and it is partly because of the strange relation between life and work that Colette's literary career was unique. It was, first of all, a very long career. Colette's first novel, *Claudine à l'Ecole*, was published in 1900. Her last major work, *Le Fanal bleu*, was published in 1949. During the almost half-century between these two books, Colette steadily wrote and evolved. But with the publication and immediate success of her novel *Chéri*, in 1920, Colette's reputation as a novelist was firmly established. Her later works, different in tone and scope, were perhaps not fully appreciated because of the fact that Colette was known mainly as a novelist, as the creator of Claudine and Chéri. Moreover, in the public mind she herself was stamped as belonging to the world of her characters.

The most important single factor which long made it almost impossible to have an over-all picture of Colette's work was that, until 1949, many of her writings were difficult to find. They had been brought out by different publishers, and many of her shorter articles had been printed only in small brochures and newspapers. With the competent aid of Maurice Goudeket, her third and last husband, Colette went over all her writings, wrote prefaces and established order, and in 1948–1950, Flammarion published in fifteen volumes the *Oeuvres complètes de Colette*.

An extraordinary phenomenon, both as a woman and as a writer, Colette defies most traditional classifications. The incidents and general orientation of her life, the particular quality and tone of her work, have long beguiled her readers. This woman acted in the music halls of Europe, operated her own beauty salon, patiently cultivated her garden, adored garlic and cats. She had three husbands and many lovers. To her, in their letters and messages, the young women of France turned for good advice, for practical wisdom.

This writer, in the century of Freud, wrote of her blissfully happy childhood, of her intense and yet simple love for her mother. In a period of wars and revolutions, she refused to "commit" herself. So very intelligent and so very French, nonetheless she never indulged in intellectual play, never engaged in discussions on the meaning of man or life. And though her work is considered by some to belong to the great French classical tradition, it remains outside the literary schools and fashions of the twentieth century and has almost no direct or even indirect literary or philosophical sources.

Born in 1873, Colette is of the same generation as Proust, Gide, Valéry, Péguy, Claudel and Alain, the writers who were to bequeath to our century many of its intellectual and artistic achievements and dilemmas. With the first three of these men, Colette had brief contacts. She was a great admirer of Proust's work, and one of the first in France to have an intuition of its greatness. Proust admired Colette, too, and after he had read one of her lesser novels, *Mitsou ou comment l'esprit vient aux Filles* (1919), he wrote to Colette, praising certain passages though not hesitating to criticize others.[5] Colette met Proust two or three times and wrote two very vivid descriptions of the "tottering young man of fifty. . . ."[6] Her personal contacts with Gide and Valéry were even fewer. Gide and Colette never had anything to say to each other, but Gide did write a laudatory letter[7] to her after the publication of *Chéri*, and he mentions her, always with praise, in his *Journal*.[8] With

Valéry, Colette on one occasion discussed her métier.[9] But Colette's work developed in silence. No literary talks preceded her writing, no philosophical or aesthetic views suggested a topic.

However, an author is never completely outside his own times. Certain themes which are found in Colette's work, the role of the mother, of memory, of childhood and adolescence, like certain literary problems with which her work confronts the critic—her "classical" style, the complex relation of author to narrator—find an echo in the works of her contemporaries.

Although Colette had really no "literary" relationships, certain French literary and artistic figures, Marguerite Moreno, Marcel Schwob, Anna de Noailles, Léopold Marchand, Germaine Beaumont, Hélène Picard, Luc-Albert Moreau, Francis Carco, Jean Cocteau, were her very good friends. It is interesting to note that Colette's correspondence, like her friendships, is almost completely personal and non-literary. She refused to discuss literature in general, as she refused to write about anything in general.[10]

Colette, very far removed from the intellectual-aesthetic atmosphere in which the "greats" of her generation lived and created, was also very far removed from the generation of Malraux, Camus and Sartre. Like these men, Colette moved in a godless world, but, unlike them, was in no way disturbed by this. Raised by her mother, Sido, to look at and to marvel at the daily miracles of nature, Colette felt no estrangement from the world around her, no anxiety, but rather delight before natural objects. Again, like Malraux, Camus and Sartre, Colette considered life an adventure. But she did not fight

against the inevitable, against the *condition humaine.*
In her work, life and death and suffering are accepted,
experienced and, in so far as it is possible, explored.
There is no metaphysical anguish in Colette's world, as
there is no deep concern with the violent political up-
heavals and catastrophes of this century. There is always, however, an implicit moral imperative, applicable, not to groups of men or to their salvation, but to the
individual in his everyday existence. This moral imperative is contained in the word *"Regarde"* which
meant to Colette, look, feel, wonder, accept, live.[11] It was
the word most often used by her mother, Sido, and it
was the last word which Colette uttered before her
death.[12]

Although she professed no general ideas about literature or life or their relationship, there is nevertheless in
her writings a new, exciting and as yet almost unex-
plored point of view on the world. The key word is
"Regarde."

 **I I**

A Partial Portrait:
Facts Deduced from Fictions

Had Colette never sat down to write, the story of her life would still bear telling. It is an intriguing, a rare story; it is even a story with a moral. It would be inconceivable outside the framework of a civilized, sophisticated society.

Perhaps the first word that comes to mind in thinking of Colette's life is the word liberty. Not that Colette enjoyed more liberty than other women of her generation, but she took advantage of that liberty which was hers, a liberty to be what she was, to do as she pleased. This Colette achieved slowly. She had first to realize what it was she wanted to be. She had then to realize that she was free. The story of Colette's life is the story of a fight for freedom, not a political, social or economic freedom, but a personal freedom—that freedom which has most meaning in terms of an individual human existence. It is unlikely that Colette consciously fought for this freedom. Had she done so, her life would surely seem more patterned, the spontaneity which characterizes her would be less apparent. But it is in the very texture of her life that this general orientation may be felt; it is in the successive incidents of her life that the development of a certain design may be perceived. With all its ups and downs and scandals, Colette's life moved in a very definite direction toward an always richer and more personal contact with the world.

Although during her last fifteen years Colette suffered from arthritis, she was basically a very healthy and vigorous woman, a woman whose physical appetites were of considerable proportions. Colette's abundant good health not only allowed her to satisfy her appetites, it also undoubtedly affected her general outlook. One of her most remarkable qualities was that she was so much at home in the physical world, that she derived so much pleasure from the simple or material joys of life: eating, walking, sleeping, making love.

It is not possible to speak of Colette as a woman of "peasant" origin, and it would be an oversimplification to claim that her country childhood was the only factor responsible for the ease with which Colette moved in the physical world. It is nevertheless true that Colette was characterized by a kind of naturalness that is rarely associated with city dwellers. Did Colette in later years work at this naturalness, develop it into a pose, a mask to be worn at public functions? Did Colette try to act a part she felt she was obliged to play? Perhaps. But if so, the mask was an exaggeration, not a creation; it corresponded to something real.

"Freedom," "health," "naturalness" are very general terms. In order to see them in operation, one must turn to certain concrete details of Colette's life.

> *I could not hide from him the jealous dis-*
> *couragement, the unjust hostility that takes*
> *hold of me when I realize that people look*
> *for me in the pages of my novels.*[1]

The problem for the biographer and the critic anxious to speak both of Colette's life and of Colette's work is a complex one.[2] It is extremely difficult to determine the division between pure autobiography and the transposed reality in Colette's writings; it is extremely easy to mingle fact and fiction in such a way that it becomes impossible to disentangle Colette's own life from the lives of her characters. What sources, then, are today available to the critic? None that are completely accurate, but many which can give, if not an untinted picture of Colette's life (and, indeed, what life retold is not in some measure tinted and distorted?), at least its tone, its atmosphere. There are the personal reminiscences of Colette's friends and enemies,[3] some of Colette's correspondence, newspaper interviews, the results of scholarly investigations and, of course, her own work. With the aid of this material a partial portrait can be drawn.

For the first thirty-three years of Colette's life, from her birth in 1873 until her divorce from her first husband, Henry Gauthier-Villars (better known as Willy), in 1906, one is obliged to lean almost exclusively on her own writings: *La Maison de Claudine* (1922), *Sido*, (1929) and *Mes Apprentissages* (1936). A few scholars and journalists have made trips to Colette's birthplace, Saint-Sauveur-en-Puisaye, and have made inquiries into her family history and school days. In general, these inquiries have added little to what Colette herself had already told. For the period of her first marriage (1893–1906), it is again necessary to rely on Colette's own writings, although several minor figures who knew Colette and Willy at the time of their marriage have left their impressions of the woman, the man and the couple. Colette's music-hall career (1906–1912) again forces one to turn to her writings, to *La Vagabonde* and *L'Envers du Music-Hall*. Some of the outstanding incidents of her career have, however, been recorded in newspapers. Less obscurity surrounds the period that begins with Colette's second marriage in 1912 and ends with her death in 1954. Claude Chauvière and Germaine Beaumont, both of whom were Colette's secretaries and protégées, have written about the Colette they knew. Claude Chauvière's *Colette* and Germaine Beaumont's articles supply us, not with factual accounts of the life of Colette, but rather with a sense of the "mystery" of her personality, of the strong attraction she exerted over others, and with ample proof of Colette's amazing vitality.

Maurice Goudeket's *Près de Colette*, although it recounts many anecdotes of Colette's life between 1925, the date of her first meeting with Maurice Goudeket, and her death, is essentially an attempt to capture the style of the woman and the writer. It is obvious that for those who knew Colette well, the woman was as fascinating as the work, and that it was impossible to divorce one from the other. Journalists who came to Colette's door begging for interviews also succumbed to the spell of her piercing eyes and her unexpected answers. Occasionally these indiscreet men asked rather personal questions about her life, questions which Colette, with good humor, amusingly answered.

Most of Colette's correspondence is as yet unpublished. But if the *Lettres à Hélène Picard* (Paris, Flammarion, 1958) and the "Lettres intimes à la confidente Marguerite Moreno" (*Le Figaro Littéraire*, July 25–August 8, 1959) may be taken as samples of Colette's correspondence, the eventual publication of the remainder may shed some light on certain obscure periods of her life. The letters to Hélène Picard, written between 1921 and 1942, and the published letters to Marguerite Moreno, written between 1923 and 1947, reveal something of the writer's relationships with her friends and the world around her, her incredibly varied activities and the role she accorded to her writing.

The reminiscences of friends and enemies, the inquiries of scholars, letters written and received, must yield to the biographer's most valuable and most dangerous source, Colette's own works. Certain of them, such as "Nuit Blanche" in *Les Vrilles de la Vigne* (1908), "L'Habitude" in *La Femme cachée* (1924), *Le Pur et l'Impur* (1932) and *Bella-Vista* (1937), suggest that there are deliberate silences, significant omissions in what Colette has told about herself. Indeed, aside from *Mes Apprentissages*, in which she speaks of the years spent with Monsieur Willy, Colette seldom speaks directly of her private life. It may be assumed that in fifty years or so, when all of Colette's friends and their immediate descendants will have died, an enterprising biographer will be able to write of the secret and many loves of Sidonie Gabrielle Colette. The story may possibly be a best seller, but it is doubtful whether such a book would in any way contribute to an understanding of Colette's work. One may venture to say now that Colette enjoyed a more varied and robust private life than most women or, for that matter, most men. But in order not to merit Colette's "unjust hostility," the biographer must move with extreme caution among her fiction and nonfiction.

It is not the purpose of the present study to set forth all the known facts of Colette's life, but rather to highlight those periods and incidents which most affected her and which, in consequence, bear directly on her work. What is important to the literary critic is not only what really happened, but what the experiences meant to Colette and the use which she, as an artist, made of them.

There are two periods in Colette's life to which, in her writings, she always returns. In these may be found the source of the major themes and symbols in Colette's work. They provide the material for both her first-person writings, which include her reminiscences and meditations and which created the image of the "stoical," "wise" Colette, and for her fiction, her tales concerning the relationships between men and women, which created the image of the "Bohemian," "demimondaine" Colette. The first period is that of her childhood and adolescence, dominated by the presence of her mother, Sido; the second is the period of her marriage, dominated by the presence of her first husband, Henry Gauthier-Villars.

III

From Saint-Sauveur to the rue Jacob

I belong to a province which I have left.[1]

Sidonie Gabrielle Colette was born on January 28, 1873, at Saint-Sauveur-en-Puisaye in the department of the Yonne. She was the last of her mother Sido's four children, and the second child of her father, Captain Jules Colette.

Her mother, Sidonie Landoy, was born in Paris in 1835, and passed her childhood in the Yonne. Sido's father, called "Le Gorille," is said to have been a quadroon; of her mother, little is known. Sido lived most of her adolescent life with her journalist brothers in Belgium. Her first marriage, to Jules Robineau, a native of Saint-Sauveur-en-Puisaye, was, despite the birth of two children, an unhappy one. Monsieur Robineau died in 1865, and the following year Sidonie Robineau became Sidonie Colette.

Jules Colette was born at Toulon in 1829. A career officer, he was wounded in Italy in 1859 and had one leg amputated. Pensioned by the French Government, he became tax collector at Saint-Sauveur-en-Puisaye.

Even from these very brief and sketchy biographical portraits of her parents, it is plain how erroneous it would be to claim that Colette descended from peasant stock. Living with her brothers in Belgium, Sidonie Landoy, Colette's mother, came in contact with many young artists and newspapermen. Her favorite authors, so Colette declares in *La Maison de Claudine*, were Saint-Simon for bedtime reading and Corneille, in Bible covering, for church. There is an aura of sophistication in the character of "Sido"[2] as Colette portrays her, which undoubtedly has its origin in the real Sido's rather worldly adolescence and in her reading. Jules Colette, always planning and rarely doing, an avid reader of such French magazines as *Le Mercure de France*, *Le Temps*, and *La Revue Bleue*, and a sentimental Sunday poet, is likewise very far removed from the French peasant of the Yonne.

Inhabitants of a comfortable house in the midst of a small French village, Colette's parents, were, at least for a time, solid members of the French petite bourgeoisie. They were also, each in his own way, strong personalities, with undeveloped literary leanings. Sido's letters[3] and the Captain's carefully bound and kept notebooks of blank pages (destined to remain blank) attest to the fact that Colette did not spring completely unheralded into the literary world.

Colette's half-sister, Juliette, her half-brother, Achille, and her brother, Léo, were strange children, and Léo retained his strangeness, his inability to live outside the world of his childhood, until his death. It is known that Juliette married and that Achille became a country doctor; but for the rest one is dependent on Colette's vivid and often weird portraits of them. Although, in later years, Colette seems to have had a marked fondness for Léo and his occasional unannounced visits, there were no close ties between Colette and her sister and brothers. They interested her rather as Sido's children and as a part of her childhood.

Seventeen years spent almost exclusively in a small French provincial village, with its simple but repeated rituals, its dramas, cannot but leave their mark. There was a bourgeois, provincial side to Colette's character which she was the first to recognize. It manifested itself by a need for an inner and outer order, equilibrium and harmony. Colette has been called the most "French" of twentieth-century writers, and the adjective refers, not only to her deep love for her country [4] and to certain qualities of her prose, but also to the influence of Colette's provincial background on the development of her character as it is reflected in her works. Recipes for cooking, for gardening and for living, abound in the pages of Colette's books and letters and betray an underlying and constant practical and moral preoccupation.

Perhaps what most characterizes a French provincial town or village and the people who inhabit it, and this despite the normal quota of bickering, crime and passion, is that it is so very civilized. Civilized in the sense that it has been lived in for centuries, that its soil has been cultivated for centuries, and that its population has inherited centuries of habits and traditions. Civilized, too, in the sense that everything, nature and buildings, which surrounds the individual seems to have been created to "fit" man, not to oppress or to engulf him. Many are the French artists and writers, who, brought up in just such a small village or town, have revolted from it and its moral and physical limitations. Colette never knew this revolt. And had not her marriage forced her to leave the provinces for Paris, it is possible that she would have been content to remain all her life in the limited but secure world they offer.

In Colette's work, there are many pages devoted to descriptions of France and its provinces, but these are extrinsic to what may be called Colette's inner and highly stylized childhood world. This childhood world is limited to a house with a high wall and a carefully tended garden, gently but firmly ruled by her mother, Sido, inhabited by her infirm, outwardly gay though inwardly sad father, her long-haired sister, her two wild brothers, the household pets, and a small, proud and happy girl, her mother's treasure, the future Colette. Into this well-defined environment wander the secondary characters, the inhabitants of the village.

Outside the family group and yet very much a part of it, playing also a principal role in the life of the child and the adolescent, is nature: the woods, the plants, the flowers, the animals which Sido knew and loved so well, and the sense of whose mystery and beauty she transmitted to her young daughter. For Sido was passionately interested in all manifestations of life; they constituted for her the only, the real miracles.

Solitary walks in the woods, listening, watching, touching, smelling were a necessary part of Colette's existence. This early and continued deep contact with nature is undoubtedly the origin of her own "passionate taste for everything which breathes in the air, free and far from man—tree, flower, frightened and gentle animals, furtive water of useless sources. . . ." [5] Nature was, for the young "queen of the earth" as it was to be for the woman, an object of study,[6] a source of peace, and it was always linked, in Colette's mind, to her childhood.

Unlike certain of the young women writing in France today, Françoise Mallet-Joris or Françoise Sagan, Colette did not, at an early age, even think of writing as a career. In "La Chaufferette," [7] Colette reveals that she never scribbled poetry, that as an adolescent she never tried to express herself in writing. "For I felt, more and more each day, I felt that I was particularly made not to write." [8] She was too busy living in the bosom of a very happy family and observing nature. "My childhood, my free and solitary adolescence, both spared from the worry of self-expression, were both involved uniquely in directing their subtle antennae toward that which can be contemplated, touched and breathed." [9] The picture of Colette derived from her multiple descriptions of her childhood is that of a very free and untroubled child, adored by and adoring her mother, full of affection for and receiving affection from her father, brothers and the household pets, a child, an adolescent fully satisfied with the life that her small provincial village offered: the warmth and security and rituals of her home, the wonders of nature. "No railroad in my native province, no electricity, no nearby college or large city. In my family, no money, but books. No gifts, but tenderness. No comfort, but liberty." [10]

Colette was, at a very early age, a voracious reader. It was not, she declares in *La Maison de Claudine* (1922), that she read so many books, but that she constantly reread those she loved. At the head of her list came Balzac. Colette began reading *La Comédie humaine* at the age of seven, and her passion for Balzac and his "jungle" was never to wane. She also read Labiche and Daudet, Mérimée, Hugo and Zola. Children's books never had any place on her literary shelf.

In the small school of Saint-Sauveur-en-Puisaye, according to her schoolmistress, Mademoiselle Olympe Terrain, Colette was a lively, intelligent pupil, always first in French composition. Her school days and the examination, the *Brevet Elémentaire*,[11] which terminated them in 1889, undoubtedly provided much of the background for *Claudine à l'Ecole*.

Colette's schooling was over when she was sixteen. She had studied French history, French literature, the geography of France and the French Empire, practical ethics, arithmetic, Euclidean geometry, algebra, elementary facts about the natural sciences. No classical or modern languages were included in the program of the *Brevet Elémentaire*. The emphasis was most definitely on France. There was school, and there was also Sunday School. But just as God appears only once or twice in Colette's writings, so her religious training receives only one mention. Colette speaks of herself as a child "who instinctively ennobled with paganism the Christian holidays," [12] a child superstitiously attached to the concrete objects that symbolized religious feasts, the Easter eggs, the pancakes, the flowers. After her First Communion, Colette's ties with the church were broken.

The real and lasting lessons which Colette learned so well came neither from books nor from school, but from her mother and that quality of inner peace which Sido transmitted to her family. "Perhaps our neighbors imitated, in their gardens, the peace of our garden where children never fought, animals and humans expressed themselves softly, a garden where, during thirty years, a husband and a wife lived without raising their voices." [13] Sido allowed her children the maximum of liberty, always watching them a bit anxiously from afar with the maximum of love. Great, too, were Sido's love and affection for her ever jealous and passionate husband, Jules Colette. Attached to the village in which she lived, Sido was nevertheless partially separated from its inhabitants by her way of life, her original system of values. Colette, in a chapter of *Aventures quotidiennes* (1924) entitled "Progéniture," tells of the sorry lot that awaited illegitimate babies and their young mothers in her village.

> My mother, loving protectress of all beginning life, did her best to save the still secret child. Twice, she took in her household unwed mothers-to-be and her only words to them were "Take off your corset, my child." A limited morality? My little province judged it limited, that morality too big for it.[14]

Indeed, Sido's notions of right and wrong were often in contradiction with the generally accepted moral tenets of her milieu. For Sido, as later for Colette, nothing in nature was evil. Everything was worthy of her curiosity, her attention and her love.

Despite her quarrels with the priest and her irreligion, Sido went regularly to church on Sundays, possibly for the same reason that, censuring marriage even more than divorce, she nevertheless had two husbands. "I had to . . . one belongs to one's village." [15] Sido's immense pity for and willingness to help any suffering living thing despite her physical repulsion in the presence of sickness and death, the constant care and attention she gave to her four children and her infirm husband despite her own ailments and financial worries, form one side, the "Christian" side of Sido's complex personality. But the round, short woman who, throwing back her head toward the clouds, cried out, as if to them, "Where are the children?" [16] and who, alone in the garden at night, mimed the sufferings of her elder daughter in labor, is a very mysterious, almost primitive goddess of the earth.

If, as Colette grew older, the figure of Sido was to be more and more present in her thoughts as in her work, it was not only because Colette deeply admired and loved her mother, or because she learned from her more than from any other single source, but also because the aging and eventually ailing Colette came to resemble Sido so closely.

This period of childhood and adolescence became for Colette the equivalent of a paradise in which she had moved free and pure, for this paradise was lost, and her rupture with it was brutal. In 1890, Jules Colette's inability in money matters plunged the family into severe financial difficulties. Their furniture was auctioned and the family moved from Saint-Sauveur-en-Puisaye to the village of Châtillon-Coligny. There Colette was to meet and very much love Henry Gauthier-Villars (Willy), fifteen years her senior, the son of a onetime acquaintance of her father. Colette and Willy were married in 1893. When she married Willy and went with him to Paris, Colette changed worlds. Not only did she move from the country to the city, from a house and woods to a small airless apartment on the rue Jacob, she moved also from a free yet well-regulated way of life into a Bohemian Paris milieu of the 1890's, from a paradise of purity and freedom into a purgatory of hypocrisy and suffering. Colette later spoke of this break with her past as a time when "I had to leave both happiness and youth." [17]

 # IV

From the rue Jacob
to the Palais Royal

> *My life as a woman begins with this adversary. A serious meeting for a village girl. Before him, everything—except for the ruin of my parents and the furniture sold in public—was roses. But what would I have done with a life of roses.*[1]

The thirteen years which Colette spent with her husband, Willy, from 1893 until their divorce in 1906, were varied, difficult and invaluable ones. In *Mes Apprentissages*, written as late as 1936, Colette, with her usual reserve and distance, gives an interesting if incomplete picture of this period of her life and of those people and events which entered into it.

Gay Paris of the 1890's, the Bohemian Paris, the Paris of the Moulin Rouge, of late supper parties, of opium smokers and homosexuals, of fast living newspapermen, of farces, quips and anecdotes, of erotic literature that would sell, the Paris of the *Belle Epoque*, this was the Paris in which Willy lived and to which he introduced his young wife. "The so-called Bohemian life always suited me as badly as feathered hats or dangling earrings." [2] This Bohemian life for which Colette felt so little attraction was, nevertheless, to provide her with the characters and décor for many of her works, and Colette, in turn, helped through her writings to provide it with an almost certain immortality.

Colette, at twenty, with her long braids and her innocent, country air, accompanied by her rotund, gregarious husband, became a familiar figure at the Parisian theaters, concerts and cafés, and in the literary circles which Willy frequented. On Saturdays, the couple could be found at the home of the poet, Heredia, on Sundays, in the salon of Madame Arman de Caillavet, on Tuesdays, at the offices of the *Mercure de France*, where Rachilde, novelist and critic, reigned supreme. During these thirteen years, Colette was to make many friends: the writer, Paul Masson, "the first friend of my married life"; [3] the essayist, poet and novelist, Marcel Schwob, who came regularly to visit Colette during her one serious illness and who read to her from his works and translations; his wife, the actress, Marguerite Moreno, perhaps Colette's oldest and most faithful friend; the two young writers, Pierre Veber and Jean Lorrain. She met such well-known figures of the period as the poet and novelist, Pierre Louÿs; the composer, Claude Debussy; the playwright, Courteline; the writer, Catulle Mendès; the poetess, Renée Vivien; the American patroness of the arts, Nathalie Clifford-Barney; the socially prominent woman of letters and of women, the Duchesse de Clermont-Ton-

nerre. But her contact with these friends and acquaintances, her everyday life, spent for the most part alone
in the apartment on the rue Jacob and later the rue de
Courcelles, were entirely subordinate in importance to
the influence and presence of her enigmatic husband,
Monsieur Willy.

> *What should be written is the story of that
> man. The difficulty is that no human being
> knew him intimately.*[4]

Several books, hundreds of articles, have been written
about and around the strange figure of Monsieur Willy.
At the turn of the century, he was one of the best-known
personalities of the much-publicized Paris literary
world. If today he is known chiefly as Colette's first husband, at the time of their marriage and almost until the
end of it Colette was known as Monsieur Willy's wife.
Indeed Willy was so well-known that in 1904 Sacha
Guitry could write: "And I know of only God and perhaps Alfred Dreyfus who are as well-known as he." [5]

Praised by his own friends and colleagues, assailed by
the defenders of Colette, Monsieur Willy remains a per-
plexing figure. It is almost impossible to judge his
"work," and it is unfair, indeed unnecessary, to judge
the man. He is important in literary history as the im-
presario of a period, the master of the pun and the men-
tor and manager of Colette.

Henry Gauthier-Villars was born on April 10, 1859,
at Villiers-sur-Orge in the department of Seine-et-Oise.
His father was the prominent Parisian publisher, Albert
Gauthier-Villars. Willy attended the Lycée Condorcet
and the Collège Stanislas in Paris and was apparently

quite well versed in Greek and Latin letters and in the music of Wagner. His first literary endeavor was a group of sonnets published in 1878. Very quickly, through his father's contacts and through his school friends, Willy gained access to the fantastic literary world that came into being in Paris in the 1880's. His sonnets were followed by a study of Mark Twain (1884) and then by an avalanche of articles and books, signed most often with one of Willy's many pseudonyms and written by God knows whom. Willy specialized in buying talent.

The purported author of numerous poems, novels and critical studies, an indefatigable journalist, a theatrical producer, Willy frequented many of the outstanding literary salons, cafés and restaurants of the period. He was the most often caricatured man about town, and an avid connoisseur of erotica. The titles of "his" novels are significant: *Une Passade (A Short Liaison), Maîtresse d'esthètes (Mistress of Esthetes), Lélie, fumeuse d'opium (Lélie, Opium Smoker), La Maîtresse du Prince Jean (The Mistress of Prince John).* A fighter of duels, a sought-after and seeking Don Juan, Monsieur Willy personified the excessive energy of the *Belle Epoque.* Everyone knew Willy, and Willy knew almost everyone who was anyone. When one of "his" novels, *La Maîtresse du Prince Jean*, written by Léon Passurf, was condemned as immoral, Willy's lawyer was a young man, Paul Boncour, later President of the National Assembly, and his witnesses were no less prominent figures than Huysmans, Funck Brentano, Catulle Mendès, Camille Erlanger.

Willy's love of a pun, particularly of a pun which ridiculed, led to rather frequent duels: with the poet, Ferdinand Herold, with James de Mitty, with Samuel Larray. One of Willy's most famous "scenes" took place during the performance of a Beethoven symphony. Erik Satie, the avant-garde composer, accused Willy of having treated him harshly in the newspapers. Willy jokingly retorted to Satie's recriminations. Satie struck at Willy with his fist and missed. Willy beat Satie with his cane. The guards separated them and Satie was taken to the police station. For most of his life, Willy came out of these skirmishes unscathed. Posterity, however, was to be less kind.

The battle cry of Monsieur Willy's apologists, Albert Henri, Jean de la Hire, Eugène de Solnière, was that Willy was always misunderstood and unappreciated.[6] These men, all friends of Willy's, have much the same things to say about him. They praise, without reserve, his vast culture, his talent, his goodness, his joviality, the complexity of his personality and, of course, his immense work. One wonders, when the last bouquet has been thrown, how much faith one can have in the sincerity of these writers. They surely knew what is now widely known, that almost every work signed by Willy was written by someone else, by one of Willy's ghost writers or *nègres:* Pierre Veber, Jean de Tinan, Curnonsky, Marcel Boulestin, Léon Passurf, Raymond Bouyer and, last and most important, Colette herself.

Excluding, for the moment, what Colette tells of Monsieur Willy, there are two writers who seem to give an unbiased view of the man and his "work." Writing in 1907 on the *Cas Willy*, Ernest-Charles says of him, "And everything in his *literary* life is publicity." [7] Monsieur Ernest-Charles attacks Jean de la Hire for his exaggerations and notes that Willy is interested almost exclusively in commercial and therefore immoral literature. Perhaps even more unbiased are the comments of J. H. Rosny Aîné. He speaks of Willy as egotistical and cruel, but insists on Willy's "incontestable charm," his "varied culture," his "real talent," and concludes by saying that Willy possessed "a wealth of knowledge which his indolence never allowed him to deepen." [8]

It is much to Colette's credit, for she was hardly an unbiased outsider, that when she speaks of Monsieur Willy in *Mes Apprentissages* she, too, recognizes his talent and his misplaced and unused abilities. " 'The Willy problem' is unique: the man who didn't write had more talent than those who wrote in his name and place." [9] And she speaks from personal experience when she writes that Willy had "a stimulating manner of criticizing, and the habit of judging without over-generously recompensing. . . ." [10]

Monsieur Willy is much less liberal when he speaks of Colette. He praises *Les Dialogues de Bêtes* (1904), the first work Colette wrote to which she was able to sign her own name, and then adds "Ah! if only she were less lazy." [11] When one realizes that this comes from a man who literally locked his wife in the room where she wrote for him, it is difficult to accept the statement as made in good faith, and yet it is quite possible that at first Colette was lazy, at least with regard to writing.

Despite the peculiar circumstances which surround the many works signed "Willy," it is nevertheless possible to distinguish among them and to determine the kind of literature Willy wanted to write and the way he wanted it to be written. There exists a book called *Sou-*

venirs littéraires et autres (1925), signed "Willy" and written in the first person. It would seem as if this book were written by Willy himself, for the style and the tone are very close to the excerpts from Willy's letters which Colette quotes in *Mes Apprentissages*. Colette states that Willy's correspondence reveals "the refusal to write." [12] Among the examples she gives is this passage from a letter sent by Willy to one of his ghost writers:

> Construct for me small chronicles with dialogue, as short as you can, fifteen lines, about some little inexpensive dump. Illustrate them with Marcel Ballot, Marquis de Chasseloup-Laubat, Frank Richardson, famous English essayist. Willy accompanying sumptuous English women, one of whom makes her bathing suit split and the Kodaks click. Anemic baccarat, forty francs against the bank, two rival casinos. Important: "Her husband ran off with a girl named Maud. She followed him.—Bravo! That's a ménage à la Maud!" (or: which follows la Maud).[13]

Souvenirs littéraires et autres yields a brief portrait of the man, sketches of his contemporaries, his personal views on music and love. The style is almost telegraphic; it is as if the author were unable to write a full sentence. The tone is slick and cynical, and Willy relies on rather dubious puns and obvious erotic references for his humor. Certain of his chapter headings may serve as examples:

> The Questioners and the Questioned. Gaston Picard, Jean-Bernard, Ajalbert, Divoire, etc. Sapphic correspondence of fashion magazines. The two Willys. Autobiographical octopuses. My Ancestor, the Maréchal de Villars. The Newspaper *Lutèce*. Albert Delpit cries in the arms of my cousin and urinates in his trousers.[14]

Here as elsewhere, Monsieur Willy refers to himself as

"*Le père des Claudines*," or he uses one of his numerous pseudonyms: Robert Parville, Jim Smiley, Boris Zichine, *l'Ouvreuse*,[15] Henry Maugis. The latter is the best known and the most revealing of Willy's assumed names.

Monsieur Willy's need for publicity, his need to be seen and to be known, also expressed itself in the myriads of photographs and portraits which he had made of himself. The creation of the fictional character Henry Maugis is the most extreme manifestation of this need. Monsieur Willy himself was responsible for the initial creation of Henry Maugis, who makes his first appearance in the second volume of the *Claudine* series, *Claudine à Paris* (1901) and who thereafter reappears in all the novels which, though written by Colette, were signed by her husband. Maugis also appears in other novels signed "Willy" and written by his many other *nègres*. *Suzette veut me lâcher*,[16] one of the novels in which Henry Maugis plays a major role, is of particular interest. The first line of the novel not only establishes the atmosphere, but also reveals Monsieur Willy's influence and his peculiar taste: "Why are you putting on your pants again, Countess?" This novel is mainly a pretext for the relating of erotic anecdotes, but it is interesting because certain of the characters evoked in its pages are the same as those who appear in the *Claudine* series: Claudine, Renaud, Rézi, Marthe Payet, Calliope Van Langendock. Although Colette did not succeed in making of these "imposed" characters successful literary creations, they are nevertheless portrayed with more humor and more delicacy in the novels of the *Claudine* series than in this novel with which Colette had nothing at all to do.

Henry Maugis seems to be a portrait of Willy as he saw himself or as he would have liked to see himself. In either case, neither the image nor the ideal is particularly attractive. In *Mes Apprentissages*, Colette, who obviously disliked Maugis, gives Willy due credit for his creation.

> This Maugis "aflame with paternal vice," amateur of women, of exotic alcohols and puns, musicologist, hellenist, scholar, fighter, sensitive, without scruples, who smirks while hiding a tear, juts out a bullfinch stomach, calls little women in chemises "my baby," prefers the deshabille to the naked and socks to silk stockings—this Maugis is not my creation.[17]

Maugis, the alcoholic, loud-mouthed and talented literary critic known to all, an eternal seeker of new mistresses, a rabid anti-Semite, seems to be a transposed but nonetheless essentially faithful caricature of Monsieur Willy. This, then, is the man who was not only to start Colette on her literary career, but who was also to introduce her to love and "the laborious, the exhausting sensual pastime." [18] This was the man who, temporarily, at least, was to replace Sido as the dominant presence in Colette's life.

> *Mon Dieu! how young I was, and how I loved that man! and how I suffered.*[19]

This confession, this cry of pain, is uttered by one of Colette's characters, Renée Néré, in the novel *La Vagabonde* (1911). Speaking in her own name, Colette never reveals intimate details of her private life; she suggests

them or she uses the more general third person, speaking
for all humanity or all women. But Renée Néré, although a character in her own right, bears certain striking resemblances to her creator. She, too, marries a well-
known man, and she, too, early discovers her husband's
multiple infidelities; she, too, finds herself plunged into
the endless and useless torments of jealousy and suspicion.

Colette was married to Monsieur Willy at the age of
twenty, but she had known him since she was sixteen
and she was engaged to him when she was eighteen. The
force of attraction which a young country girl, still an
adolescent, could feel for an older, mature man is admirably described by Colette in *Mes Apprentissages*.
Characteristically, the passage begins with the subjective first person and changes to the more general and
more objective third person.

Will people understand that the fact of changing my lot
as a country girl for the life that I led from 1894 on is an
adventure sufficient to dishearten a child of twenty, if it
doesn't bore her? With the help of youth and ignorance, I
had indeed started with semi-intoxication, a guilty semi-
intoxication, a frightful and impure adolescent outburst.
They are numerous, the barely nubile young girls, who
dream of being the spectacle, the plaything, the libertine
masterpiece of a mature man. It is an ugly desire which
they expiate when they fulfill it, a desire which goes together with the nervous disorders of puberty, the habit of
nibbling chalk and charcoal, of drinking tooth powder
water, of reading dirty books and of digging pins into the
palm of one's hand.[20]

Colette is not an apologist either for herself or for the
other "young girls" who confuse, in their ignorance,

love and the imperious commands of the senses. If Colette, despite Willy's infidelities, remained with him for thirteen years, it was in part, at least, because she reveled in her role of "plaything, the libertine masterpiece of a mature man."

From the portraits and photographs of Monsieur Willy and from what is known about him, it is difficult to visualize him as a seducer and tormenter of women. But Colette was not the only one to feel his charm and to suffer from it. "The extraordinary man whom I had married possessed the gift, had mastered the tactics of occupying without rest a woman's thoughts, the thoughts of many women, of imprinting, of leaving, of keeping alive a mark that could not be confused with other marks." [21] Sexual prowess and the fear he instilled in others seem to have been the principal weapons of this bald, bearded and round Don Juan.

An anonymous letter, a visit to the scene of the rendez-vous between Willy and Charlotte Kinceler, and Colette's long "expiation" began. This period of her life was spent in suffering, in trying to hide her suffering from the piercing eye of her mother, in trips with her "tormenter" to Saint-Sauveur, to Belle-Isle-en-Mer, to Bayreuth. Spent also in long hours of solitude and enforced writing in Paris or at *Les Monts Boucons*, a house bought by Willy in Franche-Comté, this was nevertheless an "instructive period, [of] application, humility." [22] Colette lost her "girlish character, intransigent, beautiful, absurd," [23] but she slowly acquired "my most positive art . . . the domestic art of knowing how to wait, to conceal, to pick up the crumbs, to reconstruct, repaste, regild, to change an impossible situation into a possible one, to lose and regain in the same instant the frivolous taste for living." [24] Colette was learning how to live without happiness: to the wisdom of Sido was added the newfound wisdom of Colette. "Beatitude teaches nothing. To live without happiness, and not perish, there is an occupation, almost a profession." [25]

Finally, it was Willy who suggested that they separate, and in 1906, they were divorced. Willy is present, though indirectly, in all Colette's novels, in which a man and a woman, two enemies who can live neither together nor apart, enact in a closed room or house the eternal battle of the sexes.

It is difficult to believe that if Willy had not suggested that Colette write recollections of her school days, she would probably never have written at all. The fact is that a year or so after their marriage, Monsieur Willy, always in need of money, did make the suggestion, and so Colette, having bought notebooks which resembled those she had used in school, began to set down her girlhood memories. Willy read the finished product, decided that it wasn't what he wanted and put it away in a desk drawer. Two years later, while arranging his papers, he rediscovered the manuscript, reread it and concluded that with a little spice added to it the novel would sell. In 1900, *Claudine à l'Ecole* was published and signed "Willy." Its immediate success was such that Monsieur Willy ordered another novel and another, locking his young wife in a room for four hours every day to make sure that she would work. Coerced into writing, Colette slowly discovered that it could be a means of earning money (the 300 francs a month which Willy gave her as pocket money), and also that it was habit forming; soon she deliberately chose to spend certain hours of each day with pen and notebook. Thus one of France's most prominent writers began as a slave to literature and ended as an addict. French literature owes an unpayable debt to Monsieur Willy.

If knowledge of these two periods of Colette's life and the two main figures who dominate them is essential to an understanding of her work, this does not mean that the very rich and varied life she was to lead from 1906 until her death in 1954 remained without echoes in that work. Her career as a mime in the music hall from 1906 to 1912, her second marriage in 1912 to Henry de Jouvenel, her experiences as a journalist and a mother during the first World War, her many friendships and liaisons, her summers in Brittany, her trips to Italy and North Africa, her second divorce in 1924 and her third marriage, to Maurice Goudeket, in 1935, her short career as a beautician, the second World War, her old age and severe arthritis, all find a place in her stories, articles, chronicles and reminiscences. But they are, so to speak, factors incorporated into the pre-existing world the foundations of which had been laid by Sido and Willy. Childhood had been a paradise, and Sido had opened the door to it with her insistent *"Regarde"*; Monsieur Willy had destroyed that paradise, but he had, paradoxically, introduced Colette to a discipline that would lead to its rediscovery, the difficult but rewarding discipline of creative writing.

> *Everything keeps me here. But the swallow does not know that it will leave in autumn.*

*Why would I surpass, in wisdom, the most
migratory of birds?* [26]

It is curious that a woman who was herself as strong and
domineering a personality as Colette should have spent
almost all the first thirty-three years of her life under
the influence of such strong and domineering personalities as Sido and Willy. One might have expected a contrary result—a timid, clinging, effaced Colette. It can
only be supposed that under the tutelage of Sido, Colette had developed sufficient inner strength to withstand
certain of Monsieur Willy's pressures and that under the
tutelage of Monsieur Willy, she had developed talents
which were to free her from a dependency on people.

Before her divorce from Monsieur Willy, Colette
wrote four novels, *Claudine à l'Ecole*, *Claudine à Paris*,
Claudine en Ménage and *Claudine s'en va*, two short
stories, *Minne* and *Les égarements de Minne*, and one
short book of animal dialogues, *Les Dialogues de Bêtes*.
After her divorce from Monsieur Willy, Colette was
obliged to earn her own living. It did not at that time
appear to Colette, known only as the author of *Les Dialogues de Bêtes*, that she could make her living as a
writer, and so she turned to a profession for which she
had some talent and some experience, the music hall.

It was Monsieur Willy who had first introduced Colette to the Parisian theater and theater life of the early
1900's. Involved in all kinds of literary activity, Willy
directed the production of *Claudine à Paris* (1902) star-
ring Polaire, a favorite of the Parisian music-hall world
who was famous for her thin waist, her convulsive movements, her melancholy eyes and her foreign accent. The

music hall, with its exuberant gaiety, its lavish costumes, flourished during the *Belle Epoque*. From 1885 to 1913, La Goulue, then Mistinguett, then Yvette Guilbert reigned supreme in the music halls and thus in Paris. Colette was not a very brilliant star in the music-hall firmament. It is as chronicler rather than as mime that her name is inextricably linked to this extravagant world. First immortalized at the end of the nineteenth century by the paintings of Toulouse-Lautrec, the music hall lives on in the stories and chronicles of Colette.

Colette's own acting career started when she married Monsieur Willy. His need for publicity included the need to publicize those around him, and Colette was often made to act a part. Struck by the resemblance between Polaire and his wife, Willy created his "twin" daughters and delighted in attending first-night performances with a twin on each arm. Willy's many infidelities also gave Colette ample opportunities to play different roles: the jealous wife, the sophisticated wife who entertained one mistress while Willy was busy with another, the contented wife when Sido came to visit.

Colette's first appearance as an actress, in 1903, is surrounded by an atmosphere of ambiguity. Monsieur Willy's relentless curiosity had brought him into contact with certain Parisian homosexual groups. To one of these groups, exclusively feminine, Willy introduced Colette, Polaire and his mistress of the moment, Meg Villars. The unofficial head of this particular group was the daughter of the Duc de Morny, a woman recently separated from her husband, the Marquis de Belboeuf, and known to her friends as Mitzy. Like her companions,

Mitzy dressed in tailormade suits from London and had
artistic pretensions. She had written the outline of an
oriental pantomime, *Le Rêve d'Egypte*, and was in need
of an actress. Mitzy consulted Willy and he suggested
his wife.

It is not the intention here to dwell too long on Colette's relation to this group or to its leader. Monsieur
Bonmariage has insisted in his book, *Willy, Colette et
Moi*, that Colette did have love affairs with Mitzy, with
Polaire and indeed with a considerable number of
women. Be that as it may, the fact is that Colette did not
decline an offer which was to bring her into very close
contact with this coterie.

Due to her love of gymnastics, bicycles and horses,
Colette was, in 1903, very supple. But she knew nothing
about either pantomime or the dance. And so, to teach
his wife, Willy engaged a young, talented mime,
Georges Wague. The lessons were apparently quite extraordinary, for Colette, despite much good will, was
incapable of following directions. Wague's comment on
his pupil was that she lacked experience, but that her
gestures were unforgettable. Colette was hailed as a success in *Le Rêve d'Egypte*, and she was invited to perform
before several small private groups. One of the most
famous of these performances took place in the garden
of Miss Nathalie Clifford-Barney, a wealthy American
living in Paris. On this occasion, Colette and an American actress interpreted Pierre Louÿs' *Dialogue au soleil
couchant*. As Colette's nervousness increased, her rolling
r, common to those who come from the region of Bur-
gundy, became more and more pronounced. The author,
who was present, later informed Colette that the per-

formance had been an unforgettable experience for him
—"the unforgettable experience of hearing myself interpreted by Mark Twain and Tolstoi." [27]

The name Colette Willy, which Willy had done so
much to publicize along with his own, attracted young
authors of mime dramas. But Willy, who was managing
his wife's theatrical career as he managed her writing
career, was waiting for something unusual. The something unusual was an offer by Francis de Croisset to have
Colette appear, as a faun who pursued nymphs, in his
mime drama, *Le Désir, l'Amour et la Chimère*, at the
Théâtre des Mathurins. Willy took care of the publicity.
Rarely was a well-known actress as much on display in
newspapers and reviews as was the debutante Colette in
the weeks preceding the opening. Colette herself worked
hard and was always the first to arrive at rehearsals.
Both her efforts and Willy's were rewarded. Again Colette was a success, and she was invited to act in a gala
evening performance in Brussels.

Perhaps Colette's greatest triumph was that in 1906,
after her divorce from Monsieur Willy, Lugné-Poë, the
famous director of the Théâtre de l'Oeuvre, engaged her
for a small role in a play called *Paniska*. Colette came
on in the last act, almost naked, at the head of a Dio-
nysian procession. But it was another performance that
was to assure her of a *succès de scandale*. In January,
1907, Colette and Mitzy appeared together at the Moulin Rouge in *Le Rêve d'Egypte*. A sparseness of costume
and a rather prolonged kiss caused violent reactions
among certain male spectators who were probably
closely related to Mitzy. The stage was littered with objects, and the performance was disrupted. The next day

Colette's teacher, Georges Wague, replaced Mitzy, and the name of the pantomime was changed to *Le Songe d'Orient.*

Georges Wague was to remain Colette's partner until the end of her career as a music-hall mime. Together they played in various theaters throughout France and the rest of Europe. The general consensus among the critics who wrote of Colette as mime was that her talents were mediocre but that she did have a kind of magnetism which intrigued the spectators. Despite constant moving about and the strain of public appearances, Colette managed both to do her job and to write. *La Retraite sentimentale* was published in 1907, *Les Vrilles de la Vigne* in 1908, *L'Ingénue libertine* in 1909, and *La Vagabonde* in 1911. Colette's first play, *En Camarades*, a two-act comedy about adultery and adulterers, was written in 1908 and produced at the Théâtre des Arts in Paris in 1909 with Colette herself in the stellar role. On December 2, 1910, she began her long association with the newspaper *Matin*, an association which was to last until 1923. A certain pattern of living was established during this period. Writing was one activity among others. It was almost never the only activity.

Colette was thirty years old when she became a mime. It was not the first time in her life that she was forced to work regularly and to meet often arduous commitments. Writing for Monsieur Willy had accustomed her to the necessity of doing a job both quickly and well. That "the show must go on," that the actress must always be ready to smile and to perform, was not new to Colette. She had made this rule her own during the period of her marriage to Willy. Thus, Colette's six years in the music hall reinforced an already existing tendency. All her literary activity is strongly marked by the belief that a work undertaken must be accomplished to the best of the writer's ability, whether it be a novel, a newspaper article or an advertisement. This accounts, in part, for the consistently excellent style of the fifteen volumes of Colette's complete works.

In 1912, Colette married Henry de Jouvenel, three years her junior, then editor-in-chief of the newspaper *Matin*, to which she had contributed stories. It may be supposed that Colette, at thirty-nine, was eager to settle down and was perhaps amused at the prospect of changing from the world of the music hall to a world in which she would be Madame de Jouvenel. If Willy was a well-known figure in the Parisian literary milieu, Henry de Jouvenel was a well-known figure in journalistic and political circles, and was to have a rather successful political career. In 1921, he was elected senator from the department of Corrèze; in 1922 and 1924, he was the French delegate to the League of Nations; from 1925 to 1927, he was High Commissioner in Syria; and in 1933, he was French ambassador to Rome.

Henry de Jouvenel had some money, a good name and a castle, *Castel Novel*, near the small town of Varetz in Corrèze. From Saint-Sauveur-en-Puisaye to Willy's Paris, from the small hotels at which Georges Wague's troupe stopped to a French castle is quite a journey. No doubt Colette was conscious of the material advantages of her second marriage. But it would be unfair to assume that she did not, in the beginning, love Henry de Jouvenel. In any case, either because of his infidelities, or because of her infidelities, or because of the infidelities of both, the marriage was not a successful one. Their relationship was obviously strained a few years before her divorce in 1924, judging from the summers and other holidays which Colette spent in Brittany in the company of Germaine Beaumont, Hélène Picard, Germaine Patat, Claude Chauvière, Léopold Marchand and his wife, Miche. Colette rarely mentions her second husband in her writings.

The twelve years of this marriage were among the most active in Colette's life. Through her husband, she became literary editor of the *Matin*, and she also contributed stories, chronicles and theater reviews to the paper. As literary editor, Colette was forced into a new role, that of critic and judge.

Colette became a mother in 1913. Her daughter, Colette de Jouvenel, appears in many of Colette's writings as Bel-Gazou, a name which Jules Colette had given to his own daughter. Colette was fascinated by her young child and observed her as closely as if she were an exotic flower or animal. She was undoubtedly a loving mother, but she was an erratic one. After her divorce from Henry de Jouvenel, she saw her daughter, for the most part, during vacations—Christmas, Easter and the summer. Like her letters to Hélène Picard, Colette's letters to her daughter, some of which have been reprinted in Claude Chauvière's *Colette*, are characterized by a real interest in the person and an equally real but somewhat detached affection.

Colette was at Saint-Malo in Brittany in the month of August, 1914, when the first World War was declared. Henry de Jouvenel was mobilized, and Colette continued to write: articles for the *Matin*, collected under the title *Les Heures longues* (1917), and animal stories, collected under the title *La Paix chez les Bêtes* (1916). These two works, make it possible to trace some of Colette's wanderings during this period, and, even more important, to discern her very personal reaction to the war. Because she was a journalist and also perhaps because she was Madame de Jouvenel, Colette had a certain freedom of movement not granted the ordinary citizen in time of war. She was at Verdun in December, 1915, in the Argonne in January, 1915, in Rome and in Venice in July, 1915, in Varetz at Jouvenel's castle in July, 1916 and 1917. The political aspects of the war are never mentioned in her articles, although the Germans and Germany are occasionally referred to and harshly treated. What interested Colette was the direct effect of the war on herself, her small daughter and the people whom she met. At Verdun, for example, the greatest immediate danger in 1915 was that everyone would die of hunger, and Colette's interest centered on the small, hungry children. Until the first bomb fell, Colette watched with delight the beauty of an aerial chase, the arrival of the German planes, the attack of the French. She very aptly noted that those who are not involved in the actual fighting adapt themselves rather quickly to the inconveniences and the atmosphere of war. At the age of two, Bel-Gazou's restricted vocabulary was a war vocabulary: "Boum, Gun, Soldier."

In the summer of 1915, when she went to Italy, Colette discovered the strength of her attachment to France. Enjoyment of the beauty of Italy, the pleasure of being in Rome, in an allied capital, suddenly gave way to the realization that France was suffering, and that Colette was French. But her uneasiness was vanquished by her curiosity and by her vibrant response to the present moment. In her "Impressions d'Italie" (*Les Heures longues*), particularly in the pages on Venice, appear some of the most beautiful passages Colette ever wrote.

In *La Paix chez les Bêtes*, the war is present only in the preface. These animal stories symbolize a kind of refuge for the animals, as they are in fact a refuge for Bel-Gazou and Colette. They create a small world in which the war does not exist, from which it has been consciously excluded.

Between *L'Entrave* (1913) and *Mitsou* (1919) Colette's literary production was limited to short articles and animal dramas. The 1913–1918 period would appear the least prolific in Colette's writing career. This may be explained by the disruptive influence of the war and by the birth of Bel-Gazou. With *Mitsou*, Colette began the most abundant and perhaps the most important decade of her literary achievement. During this time Colette's journalistic activities continued. Although in 1924, she left both Henry de Jouvenel and the *Matin*, she continued to write for other newspapers. She was also in charge of the *Collection Colette*, published by Ferenczi, and in the *Lettres à Hélène Picard* there are multiple references to the literary talks given by Colette in Nice, Toulon, Avignon, Aix and Marseilles. Colette, in 1924, was fifty-one years old. The tone of her letters, however, would suggest a much younger woman. A typical letter of this period runs as follows:

69 Boulevard Suchet,   Saturday, January 12, 1924
Auteil 06–27

My little Hélène,   You [tu] must be completely baffled by
my silence and my absence. Know that I work from 8:30
A.M. to one A.M. I am dead tired. But I had to do all that I
did. Today, at 8:30 I was at my desk: an eleven-page scenario in five acts which I left at lunch, in the hands of
Léo [Léopold Marchand], the actress Sylvie and Faure.
There followed two hours of exhausting palavers. At three
o'clock I was at Mouthon's, the director of the *Journal*. He
is starting a weekly and wants to take me in. Two hours
of palavers and figures with Vatel, Pawlowski, Henri Bé-
raud, etc., etc., At five o'clock, I was on the left bank, at
Armand Colin's to whom I had sent, yesterday, the result
of a half-night's work. They are delighted, my hopes are
high. But the book has to be finished by July at the latest.
At 6:30 I was at the Maison de Blanc for a fitting, a woolen
snow suit. At seven o'clock I took the next installment of
the Journal de Colette, written last night between 10:30
and one A.M., to the *Matin*. All my days are like this. To-
morrow, Sunday, I shall be at the hairdresser's from two
to six. At seven o'clock, two ministers, if you please, Oh,
my Hélène, Klotz and Bérard are coming to get me with a
car, we are dining at Mouthon's, Seine-et-Oise. Letellier
will be there, the other director of the *Journal*, and you
know how important this is for me. Monday morning at
nine o'clock, I am going to the dentist for a bitchy molar
which has been bothering me since yesterday. Before then
I have to pack, naturally at night. My Hélène, you may
be sure that if I leave without kissing you I should be very
sad. I hope to see you Monday, I leave at eight. My address,
Hôtel Royal, Gstaad, Switzerland. Have you recovered
from the upset of the other day? I still feel remorse. I kiss
you tenderly, my Hélène

Colette [28]

Colette met Maurice Goudeket in 1925. *Mon satan classique, mon compagnon*, are the terms Colette used in referring to him in her *Lettres à Hélène Picard*. He became, in her later works, *mon meilleur ami*. In 1925, Colette was fifty-two years old, Maurice Goudeket thirty-five. Their liaison began in that year, they were married in 1935, and it may be said that they lived happily ever after, until Colette's death in 1954. Unlike Monsieur Willy and Henry de Jouvenel, Maurice Goudeket was not surrounded by any aura of glamor. He was a young man, a dilettante, full of love and admiration for Colette. From the time of their liaison until their forced separation and even beyond, Maurice Goudeket devoted himself almost exclusively to loving Colette, to caring for Colette, to propagating her work. In Colette's life he represented a solid center, a lover-husband-friend on whom she could always lean, to whom she could always turn.

In the summer of 1925, immediately following the beginning of their liaison, Maurice Goudeket introduced Colette to Saint-Tropez, a small fishing port on the Mediterranean which had not yet become a fashionable, crowded summer resort. There they bought a house, *La Treille Muscate*, to which they returned almost every summer until 1938. Like most of Colette's dwellings, *La Treille Muscate* has been immortalized in her writings. In that same summer of 1925, Colette toured the popular casinos of France, playing the part of Léa in the play *Chéri*, which, with the aid of Léopold Marchand, she had adapted from her own novel of the same title.

Colette's new relationship did not in any way change her manner of living. In Paris, during the winter, she continued to write: newspaper articles, novels and fictionalized reminiscences. In 1929, at Easter, Colette and Maurice Goudeket set out for North Africa, spending three days in Spain on the way. In 1930, they were invited by Henri de Rothschild to make a trip aboard his yacht, *Eros*, through the Norwegian fjords, and during the trip Colette worked on what was to be one of the most significant of her books, *Le Pur et l'Impur*. The trip to Spain and North Africa, like the one through the fjords, appeared in Colette's later works. The 1929–1930 crash, so disastrous in America, was not long in reaching Europe. Maurice Goudeket lost what money he had and, rather eager to give up business, turned to journalism.

In 1932, Colette, feeling that she had exhausted her literary potentiality and anxious to mingle again with ordinary people, embarked temporarily on a new career —that of beautician. It was André Maginot, the man whose name is associated with the fateful Maginot Line, who gave Colette the idea of making and selling beauty products. Colette, with her usual vigor, was most enthusiastic about the enterprise, and her beauty salon at 6, rue de Miromesnil was opened in 1932. For an entire year, Colette was actively engaged in her role of beautician: applying creams and lotions to women's faces, speaking throughout France on both "business" and literary subjects. Colette was determined that her salon should succeed, but much money and time were needed to continue the work, and a letter to Hélène Picard in January, 1933, reveals that along with her lecture tours, Colette was writing the subtitles for an American film, to be shown in France, and working on a novel, *La*

Chatte. Before the end of 1933, Colette was no longer a beautician. She had returned to her "real" profession.

Colette and Maurice Goudeket were married on April 3, 1935, and on June 4 of the same year, they were invited, as journalists, on the maiden voyage of the *Normandie.* In the two and one half days she spent in New York, Colette seems to have been particularly impressed by the objects and gadgets of American civilization. She frequented Woolworth's assiduously and made a special trip to the home of the Parker Fountain Pens. On April 4, 1936, she received what was to be the first in a rather long list of official titles; she was made a member of the Royal Belgian Academy of Letters, in the place of the recently deceased poetess, Anna de Noailles. Her acceptance speech was a memorable one, not only because she succeeded in creating an unforgettable portrait of Anna de Noailles, but also because it is quite obvious that Colette was not impressed by Anna de Noailles' poetry and she managed, without in any way belittling her predecessor, never to say what she didn't think.

In November, 1938, Colette and Maurice Goudeket were sent by the newspaper *Paris-Soir* to Fez, to report on a famous murder trial. This was to be one of Colette's last trips outside of France and marks the end of a period of extraordinary physical energy and activity, for it was some time in 1938 that Colette began to complain of pains in her right hip. The arthritis which was eventually to immobilize her completely had begun. It almost coincided with the fall of France.

In *Près de Colette*, Maurice Goudeket speaks of the years 1932–1940 as good years, as happy years, years in which, in an atmosphere of harmony, much work was accomplished. Colette's fame grew during that period. Interviews, questionnaires, letters—Colette was spared none of the paraphernalia which accompanies fame. Nor did she and Maurice Goudeket live only in their own small world. Their friendships centered in two groups: the group of artists at Saint-Tropez in the summer; the group that had as its headquarters the salon of the Princess Edmond de Polignac (*née* Singer) in Paris.

In 1940, almost everything changed. *La Treille Muscate* having been sold, Colette bought a house at Méré, not far from Paris. In the beginning of the year, her cat and her dog died, and Colette, who had never lived without animals, decided she would have no other. This was the beginning of an abdication, prompted in part by her fear that she would no longer be able to give her animals sufficient exercise. As the German menace became increasingly apparent, Colette, in her role as French housewife, and also because she had lived through the first World War, began to gather provisions. At the same time, she and Maurice Goudeket made weekly broadcasts to America, broadcasts which began at 2:30 A.M. on Mondays.

On June 12, Maurice Goudeket, Colette, and her faithful maid, Pauline, joined the exodus. From Méré, where Colette was staying, they proceeded to Corrèze, where her daughter, Colette de Jouvenel, was staying, to Lyons, which with the fall of Paris had become the active center of France and then, because Colette's attachment to Paris was so strong, back to the occupied capital.

Colette spent the war years in her Palais Royal apartment. In 1941, her *lit-divan* was placed by the window, a sign both of Colette's forced sedentary existence and her desire to watch the world. And watch she did, as she elaborated three books, half-diary, half-reminiscences: *De ma Fenêtre* (1942), *L'Etoile Vesper* (1946) and *Le Fanal bleu* (1949). The hungry children, the cold children, the households without men, the disappearance of the French Jews in her *quartier*, all this Colette noted, and she herself suffered. On the night of December 12, 1941, the Germans came to arrest Colette's husband. During the two months that Maurice Goudeket spent at Compiègne, Colette did everything she could to obtain his release, or rather almost everything, since she refused to negotiate his release on collaborationist terms. Even after Maurice Goudeket's liberation, Colette and Pauline were often alone. Fearful of being seized again by the invader, Maurice Goudeket spent most of the war years in hiding, in Paris and in the south of France.

None of Colette's fiction published during this period, *Julie de Carneilhan* (1941), *Le Képi* (1943), *Gigi* (1944), contains even a faint echo of war and occupation. Colette was continuing to build her own particular world, whose roots remained in the early years of the century.

From the end of the war until her death, Colette's reputation grew steadily. On May 2, 1945, she was elected to the Goncourt Academy, and in 1949 she became its president. She was given the Gold Medal of the city of Paris, she was made *Grand Officier* of the Legion of Honor, and the American ambassador to France presented her with the Diploma of the National Institute of Arts and Letters. *Vogue* and *Harper's* asked for stories and articles by Colette, and literarily inclined tourists in

Paris came to the garden of the Palais Royal, in the hope of seeing her at her window. When her complete works were published (1948–1950), she was "rediscovered" by the literary world. It came as a shock to many that Colette had written so much and so well. In the beginning years of the postwar period, the existentialist writers were the undisputed literary kings. Solemn, young and vigorous, they proclaimed in often weighty manifestoes the necessity of the artist's *engagement* in the world in which he lived, the solidarity of all mankind. The fifteen volumes of Colette's complete works were an efficacious antidote, both in subject and style, to the often dismal utterances of the earnest young men.

It was not only Colette's literary reputation that was growing. Colette herself, completely immobilized by arthritis, almost constantly in pain, had somehow become a symbol of France: old, suffering and having suffered, refusing to take the pills that might numb the pain and lessen lucidity, and yet gay and cheerful, her blue eyes even bluer because of the kohl in and around them, her curls still hiding her immense forehead, still eating garlic, still sipping champagne.

The last trips, by wheelchair, plane and car, to Geneva, to Monte Carlo, to Deauville—recognition and awe as she passed on the streets and in the hotel lobbies. And then on August 3, 1954, the final passage from life to death.

She was born in Saint-Sauveur-en-Puisaye; she died in Paris in the Palais Royal. For twelve years Colette lived in Saint-Sauveur-en-Puisaye, for seven years in Châtillon-Coligny, and for sixty-one years Paris was the

geographical center of her life. Each of Colette's Parisian
homes has its place in her work, from the rue Jacob on
the Left Bank, where Colette and Willy first lived, to the
rue de Courcelles, to the rue de Villejust, to the sixteenth
arrondissement, to 69, Boulevard Suchet in Auteuil, to
the Palais Royal, to the Hotel Claridge, to the Immeuble
Marignan, to 33 Champs Elysées and again and finally
to the Palais Royal. The first and the last are undoubtedly the most important. Colette was ill at ease in Willy's
small, airless apartment on the rue Jacob, and she was
too young or too unhappy to transform it into something
else. This first apartment, the center of Colette's matri-
monial pleasures and sorrows, the center, too, of her first
encounter with Bohemian Paris, represents a certain
marginal milieu to be found in many of her novels. The
Palais Royal represents the period of old age and triumph—the very harmony and beauty of the building
being somehow symbolic of Colette's own last creation,
the narrator of *L'Etoile Vesper* and *Le Fanal bleu*.

Between the two poles of Saint-Sauveur and Paris lie
the rest of France and the world. Two and one half days
in New York, a yacht trip to the Norwegian fjords, three
days in Spain, a month or so in Italy, a few weeks in
North Africa, sundry trips to Belgium and Switzerland
—Colette did travel, but rarely for pleasure. Houses
loved, bought and sold were French houses. Long vacations were French vacations: Brittany, from 1911 until
1924, and the south of France, particularly Saint-Tropez,
from 1925 to 1939, were Colette's chosen lands.

In a very short book, *Trois . . . Six . . . Neuf . . .*,
in which she speaks of her various Paris apartments,
Colette refers to herself as "migratory and sedentary,"

and these two words may be used to characterize her entire life. Sedentary, her attachment to France and to her writing, migratory, her many activities, her many loves.

Colette has been called appealing and intimidating, affectionate and calculating, stoical and flighty. She has been described as earthy and natural, sophisticated and affected, possessed of a "bronze-like" voice, a grumbling voice.[29] Critics and friends and enemies have exhausted the stock of adjectives in their descriptions of Colette. Even the many photographs, undoubtedly more objective than words, appear contradictory. Never slim, Colette became, with time, quite heavy. And, of course, between 1895 and 1950 women's styles changed constantly. But it is in the pose, the attitude of the figure in the picture, rather than in changes of style or age, that the contradictions arise: Colette holding her two cats, Colette looking at Toby-Chien, Colette writing at her desk, Colette mime, draped in a sheet, Colette with Henry de Jouvenel and Bel-Gazou, Colette with . . . Colette as. . . . So many images which correspond to so many roles: writer, mother, music-hall actress, animal lover. There is something about the woman as elusive as her style and as varied as her writings. And perhaps, after all, it is necessary to accept all the adjectives and say that Colette was appealing, intimidating, affectionate, calculating. And if she was able to play and to blend so many different roles, so many different qualities, it was because of a vitality which made her appear in whatever she did a little more than an ordinary human being.

 # V

From Colette to "Colette": Transition and Transposition

"Do you imagine in reading my books that I am drawing my portrait? Patience: it's only my model." [1]

Colette is dead, but "Colette" is still very much alive.

For approximately fifty years, at certain hours of the day, and almost every day, Colette sat down at a desk and wrote. Why did she write? In the beginning, there was Monsieur Willy. Why did she continue to write after her divorce from Monsieur Willy? Colette answered this question very simply. Writing was a means of making money, and she was often in need of money, and writing had become a habit. Why did she write what she wrote? Certain commercial firms asked her to write advertisements; a newspaper asked her to write theater reviews; her publishers wanted a novel that would sell. A large part of Colette's work, even after she left Monsieur Willy, was conditioned by demands. From what sources did she draw her material? She drew it from her childhood and Sido, from her pets, from her first marriage to Willy, from anecdotes related in her presence, from her garden, from a vase of flowers in her room, from her premonitions about the future.

Although Colette worked hard at each individual assignment or project which she undertook, it was not, in all probability, until she began rereading her works in preparation for a complete edition that she realized what it was that she had accomplished. And the extraordinary unity in so diversified an outpouring is made evident by the ease with which Colette, aided by Maurice Goudeket, could ignore chronology in the grouping and regrouping of texts.

Within unity, it is necessary to distinguish phases, aspects, themes. Colette's literary work may be divided into three parts: her fiction—novels, short stories, plays; her personal reminiscences, meditations, chronicles; and her most successful writings, which seem to defy assignment to any traditional category—those which mingle fiction, meditation, and reminiscence. How much of Colette's own life, of her own actually lived experiences and situations appear in her writing? The answer can only be an ambiguous one—very little and a great deal, or a conditional one—it depends upon which of the three aspects of her writing is under consideration.

Much of Colette's fiction and nonfiction is unmistakably rooted in autobiography, but the real events of Colette's life are arranged and disguised in such a way that it is impossible to tell at what point autobiography stops and fiction starts. The problem is similar in many ways to that which faces the critic of Proust. The narrator of

A la Recherche du temps perdu is a literary creation, an autonomous character, he is not Proust, and yet as the single voice that tells all, he is so close to Proust that the relation of author to character often becomes confusing. This is the case with many of Colette's characters.

All creators of fiction use, in varying degrees, their own personal experience as the starting point for their work. But Colette's work is very far from the kind of fiction written by a Balzac or a Dickens, involving imagined situations, a host of characters, the creation of an immense world. Almost all Colette's characters and the situations in which they are placed are traceable to real past events and known persons. The bond that links most of Colette's important female characters (and most of Colette's important characters are female) to each other and to their creator is a very intimate one. This bond between creator and character is perhaps closest in Colette's first-person novels, the five novels of the *Claudine* series, *La Vagabonde* and *L'Entrave*; Mitsou, Gigi, Léa and Julie de Carneilhan have a greater autonomy than either Claudine or Renée, although the relationship between Colette and her later heroines remains very close.

Colette's female characters may be divided into two family groups: the "Colette-Claudine" [2] branch and the "Colette-Sido" [3] branch. The "Colette-Claudine" branch comprises the adolescents or very young women: Claudine, Minne, Mitsou, Vinca, Gigi. The "Colette-Sido" branch includes the important older women: Léa, Madame Dalleray, Fanny, Alice, Julie de Carneilhan, Madame Alvarez and Aunt Alicia. The "Colette-Claudines" are directly or indirectly transposed images of the young Colette, the "Colette-Sido" transposed images of the older Colette, of the Colette who consciously or unconsciously modeled herself after her mother. These two types which dominate Colette's fictional world are even more fully realized when they are retransposed from the fictional to the "real" in *La Maison de Claudine* and in *Sido*.

This complex relationship between an author and her various characters is, as has been indicated, by no means peculiar to Colette's work, and Colette does not intentionally "play" with the idea. What is peculiar is the treatment of "Sido" and of "Colette," the author-character. Quite often, Colette does not even attempt to disguise her characters. Her mother is called "Sido"; Colette herself appears as "Colette" or "Madame Colette." But by an inverted process, in the many pages of fictionalized reminiscences, Colette's mother has become a fictional character called "Sido," and the voice that comes to us through the fifteen volumes of Colette's work, the main character, is Colette, no doubt, but a fictional "Colette."

This main character, "Colette," is little known in America, since most of the works in which "Colette" appears have not, as yet, been translated. On the other hand, some of Colette's fictional characters are extremely well known here. Of all the characters of twentieth-century French fiction, perhaps none has reached a wider American audience than Gigi. It was Colette herself who, while at Monte Carlo, in the spring of 1951, saw the then-unknown Audrey Hepburn rehearsing for a small part in a film and immediately chose her to play in Anita Loos's American stage adaptation of *Gigi*. The result was a triple success: for Colette, for Gigi, and for

Audrey Hepburn. The musical-comedy film of *Gigi*, although it contains some rather unfortunate departures from and innovations on the original text, has definitely brought Gigi and Colette to the masses. Philippe and Vinca, the protagonists of *Le Blé en herbe*, Mitsou of *Mitsou*, Claudine of *Claudine à l'Ecole* and the trio of *La Chatte* are familiar to those Americans who frequent movie houses dedicated to the showing of foreign films.

Many American magazines have, at one time or another, either printed material by Colette in translation, or reviewed translations of her works. When Colette was elected to the Goncourt Academy in 1945, and again at the time of her death in August, 1954, *Life*, with its usual splash and dash, presented a series of Colette photographs, accompanied by very short and very banal squibs. An oversimplified, biased, but saleable image of the woman, her life and her writing—Colette, the wife of Monsieur Willy, Colette, the music-hall mime, Colette, the writer of love tales—was launched in America.

It is in no way surprising that certain aspects of what *Life* called Colette's "piquant career" should have captured the public imagination. The "amoral" Frenchwoman, the young girl from the provinces who made good in Paris, these correspond to pre-existing notions about France and about success. Nor is it surprising that Gigi, Philippe, Vinca, Mitsou and Claudine have captivated movie audiences. The slim love tales in which these ingenuous if not innocent adolescents play their part are happily removed from the current portrayals of the savage, neurotic, American and French adolescent. What is surprising is how Colette managed, from her first fictional heroine, Claudine, to her last fictional heroine, Gigi, to create a type which immediately imposed itself on the reader's imagination, which seemed, despite so deliberately dated and marginal a milieu, to bear the stamp of the universal. To begin to understand "Colette," it is necessary to turn to her younger and better-known sisters.

 **VI**

From Claudine to Gigi:
Games of Love

> *"But can't you write a book that does not concern love, adultery, incestuous liaisons, separations? Isn't there anything else in life?"* [1]

The extreme subjectivity which permeates all Colette's novels provides an interesting paradox. Criticisms commonly directed against the "feminine" novelist are that she limits her novel to her own personal experience, that she is unable to create characters, that she is unable to imagine situations and that she is rarely concerned with metaphysical or moral problems. And it is true that the lineal love story has been and still is the province most explored by feminine novelists. Colette's fictional universe appears, at first, to have these limitations. Her characters are always absorbed in a love situation, and their sole concern is with this situation. There are few characters in Colette's novels, and from novel to novel similar types reappear. It is almost as if she were writing for a fixed cast of players: the adolescent, the demimondaine, the unoccupied male—people who have little else to do but to become involved with other people. But whereas this narrowing of life both to marginal social characters and to the affective part of their experience constitutes a weakness in the novels of many feminine writers, it does not constitute a weakness in the best of Colette's work.

From *Claudine à l'Ecole* to *Gigi*, each of Colette's novels presents variations and new perspectives on the theme of love. In an interview with Frédéric Lefèvre, Colette, speaking of *Le Blé en herbe*, her own favorite among her novels,[2] gives the clue to her conception of the love story:

> The history of this novel—the genesis as you scholars call it—is curious: for a long time I wanted to write a one-act play. . . . The curtain goes up, the stage is plunged in darkness, two invisible characters discourse on love with a great deal of knowledge and experience. Toward the end, the stage is lighted, and the surprised spectators realize that the partners are fifteen and sixteen years old. In that way I wanted to show that love does not have two kinds of language. I did not say anything else in *Le Blé en herbe*. I merely intercalated in the story some Breton landscapes which had vaguely moved me.[3]

It is evident that Colette conceived of her novels as dialogues or duels.[4] These dialogues or duels take place between two characters bound to each other by the tie of love. Through their dialogue, Colette intends to portray both the particularities and the generalities of the game of love. Thus, each of Colette's novels goes beyond the particular love situation and the best among them— *Chéri, Le Blé en herbe, La fin de Chéri, Duo, La Chatte,*[5] *Julie de Carneilhan, Gigi*—become parables on the nature or meaning of love. Whether the partners be a young boy and a young girl as in *Le Blé en herbe*, or a young man and an older woman as in *Chéri*, or two young women as in *Claudine en Ménage*, the game is the same and the language is the same. For each of the partners, the goal, too, is the same, to seek pleasure, joy, fulfillment, in physical love. A limited view of love, one might say, but in her novels Colette has deliberately limited love to the life of the body, or rather Colette implies that the demands of the body, by their imperious and egotistical nature, limit love. Within these limits, Colette's exploration is complete.

In each novel, the game of love is played by characters who are, for the most part, incapable of moving outside the restricted world of their sentiments, passions and illusions. The game of love condemns them to suffering or to death and endows them, common mortals though they be, with a certain grandeur. All Colette's novels might well begin with the quotation, "This book which will speak of pleasure sadly." [6]

It has often been said that Colette's male characters are weak, both as men and as characters. And if one is measuring them against a preconceived standard of virility, this charge is undoubtedly true, but the reasons for this weakness must be made clear. Colette's males are weak because her females are strong, or rather because in the love duel, as Colette saw it, the female is most often the aggressor. Colette's female characters, and to a degree that is perhaps unique, seek equality in love, equality in pleasure given and pleasure received, equality, too, in independence. Unable to live without males, they nevertheless refuse to submit to male domination. What is perhaps upsetting to the average reader is that Colette's female characters often think of and look at males in the way that, in most current fiction, males think of and look at women—as instruments of pleasure. Colette's males appear weaker, as males and as characters, because Colette has translated this notion of equality into her descriptions of them. And because, as the titles of Colette's novels indicate, the principal characters are usually female, the male becomes the love object.

Colette was certainly not a militant feminist. Similarly, it is not quite fair to see in some of her novels an exposé of the sad social and economic plight of women in the early twentieth century, although this has been done by the brilliant French communist critic, Claude Roy. Colette was both too busy and too wise to be a propagandist, too at ease with herself and the world to be a reformer. Colette's novels are "social" novels in the sense that any novel dealing with characters in a given society at a given time is of necessity "social." If it is often difficult in her novels to be a woman, the origin of the difficulty is never attributed to society, but rather to love, and Colette does not treat love as a socially determined phenomenon. There is no doubt that for Colette love must be free, but it would be an error to confuse her notion of freedom with the once much-publicized doctrine of "free love." What most of Colette's novels seem to say is that a woman is free to love, but that she is almost never free in love. But, for that matter, neither is a man.

There is still another reason for the apparent weakness of Colette's male characters. Without any solid knowledge of current psychological theorizing, Colette had by her own observations discovered the varying degrees of masculinity in women and the varying degrees of femininity in men. There is no doubt that her observations were influenced by the particular groups she frequented at a certain period in her life, and that, as a result, she tended to see a great deal of virility in women and a great deal of femininity in men. Indeed, by her recurrent use of animal and flower images, which may refer either to female or to male characters, Colette occasionally does away with male and female, and the reader is faced with an ambiguously appealing human animal. This is undoubtedly why her male adolescents are among her most successful fictional creations.

Colette remains well within the bounds of the traditional French novel. She lends her own personal experience to people who resemble her and yet are invented characters, and the story or drama in which these characters are engaged unfolds according to the conventional temporal relations between cause and effect within the framework of a carefully described society.

There is an extraordinary realism in Colette's novels, a realism of milieu and décor. Most of them are carefully dated by references to well-known personalities of a given era: Polaire, Caroline Otero, Liane de Pougy, Charles Boyer, Abel Hermant, Henri Marsan, Yvonne de Bray, Henry Bernstein, Georges Feydeau, Jean Louis Barthou, Maurice Chevalier. The milieus Colette describes are all French and all early twentieth-century: the demimondaine, the Bohemian, or the theatrical milieu described in *Claudine à Paris*, *Claudine en Ménage*, *Claudine s'en va*, *La Retraite sentimentale*, *La Vagabonde*, *L'Entrave*, *Mitsou*, *Chéri*, *La Seconde*, *Gigi* or the rather vacuous world of the bourgeois Colette evokes in *Le Blé en herbe*, *La Chatte*, *Duo*, *Le Toutounier*. The setting, save in *Claudine à l'Ecole*, *La Retraite sentimentale*, *Le Blé en herbe*, the first part of *La Seconde* and *Duo*, is an apartment in Paris, usually on the Right Bank in the sixteenth arrondissement, a confined setting which allows Colette to create a stifling atmosphere somewhat reminiscent of the *lieu unique et clos* of French classical tragedy. Rooms and their furnishings are minutely described, and the eyes, the hair, the height, the smell, the clothes, the gestures and the language of both the principal and the secondary characters are scrupulously noted. For Colette, as for Balzac, there is a direct relationship between the character and his surroundings; to describe the latter is to reveal the former.

Even if the action of the novel is set in the country, Colette so carefully delimits the terrain, so rigorously reduces to a minimum the intervention of characters exterior to the drama, that the same stifling atmosphere prevails. Only the descriptions of seasonal and climatic changes, and this, rather surprisingly, whether the scene be the country or Paris, help by their beauty to relieve the inevitable denouement. These descriptions add to the novels a sensuous texture, a poetic dimension, but they have no symbolic value. Indeed, they rarely play a role within the novel, other than to remind the reader, through the characters' sudden sensitivity to a ray of light, a bird, or a climbing honeysuckle, of the omnipresence of Colette.

Because of their brevity and their often tight construction, Colette's novels are quite easily adaptable as plays and as films.[7] They tend to be made up of a series of rigorously composed scenes, separated by a sometimes arbitrary, sometimes deliberately planned passage of time. The dramatic quality of the novels is further intensified by their objective presentation. Most of them open with dialogue, and Colette uses dialogue rather than narrative in all her crucial scenes, since the crises, in the novels, always involve the confrontation of two characters. It is through her portrayal of character that Colette comes closest to the technique of the playwright. Colette's characters are given, they are not explained; they reveal themselves through action and gesture rather than through thought. The moral truth in Colette's novels is always implicit, because it must be apprehended through the action of the novel as a whole.

When first presented, Colette's characters are already involved in a situation, something has happened before the book opens. What has happened is never a mystery, nor for that matter is why it happened. And it is not mere curiosity as to the outcome that holds the attention, but rather the desire to know how the characters will act and react. Colette's novels are psychological novels of a very particular sort.

Because Colette's novels are in literary terms, conventional in their basic situations—the jealous husband, the unfaithful husband, adolescent love—it is easy to overlook the fact that their conclusions are highly unconventional. It would indeed be difficult to find other contemporary novels in which, at the end, a wife accepts living with her husband and his mistress, young adolescents make love, heartbroken forty-year-old women return to their childhood homes.

Colette always refused to admit as intentional the moral or spiritual implications which have sometimes been drawn from her novels. It is impossible to determine whether this refusal was sincere or whether it was based, at least in part, on Colette's dislike for intellectual, abstract discussions, a dislike which, although undoubtedly real at the beginning of her literary career, seems to have developed later into a pose. If her refusal was sincere, then one can only say that for Colette, as for so many artists, creation has, in certain cases, surpassed intention. But before turning to those novels in which Colette seems to have surpassed herself, it is essential to go back to the beginning, to Colette's first novels, in order to discover what it was she had to surpass.

 # VII

Claudine and Minne

Nothing is as reassuring as a mask.[1]

Colette was, in later years, a very severe judge of her first novels and the conditions under which they were written.

> Habit does not mean blindness: I did not think that my first book was very good—nor the three which followed. With time, I have scarcely changed my mind, and I judge all the *Claudines* rather severely. They behave indiscreetly, like children and elves. Youth, certainly, blazes out, if only in the lack of skill. But it does not please me to find, if I look over some of these old books, an ease in accomplishing what was asked of me, an obedience to suggestions, and an already skilful manner of avoiding effort. . . . And I cannot forgive myself for the fact that by allusions, caricatured but recognizable sketches, plausible fables, these *Claudines* reveal a thoughtlessness in hurting others. If I am mistaken, so much the better—but I am not mistaken.[2]

When Colette wrote the *Claudine* novels, she was wearing a mask, she was writing behind the façade of

Monsieur Willy. Although she was describing certain facets of her own life, she was receiving and executing Monsieur Willy's orders. These orders all had the same purport: to create suggestive, racy novels that would sell.[3] Colette indicates in *Mes Apprentissages* those passages in the novels which were changed or arranged by Willy. He added, or rather had Colette add to her manuscript puns and patois. In these early novels, for example, there are such words as *agouant* for *exigeant* (demanding); *appleter* for *faire vite* (to do something quickly); *s'avaler* for *se tourmenter* (to torment oneself). According to Colette, Willy was responsible for the inclusion of the particular form of sensuality attributed to most of her females in the small Montigny school. However, it is quite possible that Colette's all-girls' school at Saint-Sauveur-en-Puisaye had its own share of teen-age crushes. Whether or not homosexuality was an imposed subject in the *Claudine* novels, it was a subject that Colette did not hesitate to use in some of her later, independent writings.

Colette's judgment of these first novels may serve as a guide to some of the problems that beset Colette, the novelist. So far as is known, Colette had written nothing before the *Claudine* novels, beyond the usual classroom compositions and letters to her mother. But when she was forced to write, it is evident that she wrote with ease and that, since her own name was not to appear on the book, she felt no moral or aesthetic obligation toward her work. To begin as a ghost writer is not, assuredly, the best apprenticeship for a young author. This facility in writing and this lack of responsibility for the "thing written" are both important factors in Colette's subsequent development. Colette was gradually to become more and more suspicious of her facility and consequently more and more determined that the "thing written" be of the highest quality.

The problem of the tone of these first novels is, of course, directly related to the problem of style. The "indiscretion" in caricaturing contemporaries, in barely transposing the facts and anecdotes of their lives, the lack of respect for others is a reflection of Colette's facility. In three of the *Claudine* novels, *Claudine à Paris*, *Claudine en Ménage* and *Claudine s'en va*, the vices and antics of the characters portrayed seem somewhat gratuitous and the author's point of view appears to be one of personal self-indulgence. When a temporal distance stands between Colette and this milieu, between Colette and Monsieur Willy, and as Colette grows to have a greater respect for her art, for herself, and for others, this tone of persiflage slowly disappears from her writings.

Despite Colette's retrospective severity, directed both at herself and at her husband, Monsier Willy achieved what he desired. The *Claudine* novels were tremendously successful. *Claudine à l'Ecole*, the first of the series, was almost unanimously received by the press as an outstanding novel and its author, Willy, as a great French novelist. Hailed as the *Liaisons dangereuses* [4] of the twentieth century, consecrated by the eulogies of Rachilde, *Claudine à l'Ecole* achieved the extraordinary sale of 40,000 copies in two months.

Catulle Mendès, one of the few people who immediately realized that the *Claudine* novels were written by Colette, predicted with great accuracy the fate of their

major character. "You won't be able to escape it," he
told Colette. "You have created a type." [5] Colette soon
discovered that his prediction had proved true, that she
had, indeed, created a type. There were, in the early
1900's, Claudine dresses and hats, Claudine collars for
men and women, a *glace Claudine*, a *gâteau Claudine*,
a *lotion Claudine* and even *cigarettes Claudine*. The public was evidently titillated by Claudine's combined innocence and sophistication, by the rather naïve way in
which a young girl from the provinces discoursed on and
engaged in all forms of sensual activity. Claudine was
received as another type in the literary gallery of Gallic
women, the piquant adolescent who dabbles in vice, who
tells all and who remains "pure." Her popularity was
such that she became, in certain circles, a model of feminine behavior and in others, more conservative, an in-
carnation of the devil.

What seems to have distressed Colette most of all, during this period of unprecedented success, was the constant intermingling of the names Colette and Claudine
as if they were one and the same person, a confusion
which Monsieur Willy's publicity stunts helped to
spread. Although Willy wanted to be known as the
creator of Claudine, he found it amusing that his wife
should be considered his model. In "Le Miroir," an imag-
inary interview between Colette and Claudine published
in 1908, the "real" creator is obliged to say very definitely to her domineering creation, "I am not your
twin." [6]

Colette's indictment of her first novels is certainly
valid, but for the critic these novels present an interest
other than artistic. It is perhaps a measure of the super-

ficiality of Willy's influence that these first efforts contain, explicitly or implicitly, though often in an embryonic form, the themes of Colette's future novels, the milieu in which and the characters through whom these themes are elaborated and certain essential elements of Colette's style. The happiness and innocence of childhood, the ambiguities of adolescence, the torments and pleasures of love portrayed against the background of closed rooms and agitated urban life, the soothing and healing powers of animals and nature, these are the fundamental themes of Colette's fiction. The semi-artistic, semi-Bohemian Parisian setting of the *Claudine* stories, peopled with both exotic and commonplace fauna, is, with few exceptions, the setting of Colette's later novels. The lyrical, expansive tone of the opening pages of *Claudine à l'Ecole* and the final pages of *La Retraite sentimentale*, the ironic, restrained tone of certain passages in *Claudine à Paris* and *Claudine en Ménage*, establish, at the outset of Colette's career, the two styles through which she attempts to transmit her very particular vision of reality.

Despite the presence of so many fundamental characteristics of Colette's writing in the early *Claudines*, it would be a gross exaggeration to imply that these novels convey a complete image of her work. It is true that some passages already reveal Colette's extraordinary ability to translate sensations into words without losing anything, or losing so little, of the sensation itself. But the mastery of style in *La Naissance du Jour*—a certain sense of "distance" which Colette observes while relating her most intimate feelings; the psychological subtleties of *Chéri*, *Le Blé en herbe* and *Le Pur et l'Impur*; the

poetry of *La Maison de Claudine* and *Sido* are not present or, if present, are not sustained in the *Claudine*
series.

The novels of the *Claudine* series are all written in the
first person. Four of them are presented as Claudine's
journal. Claudine notes incidents which, purportedly,
have just occurred, using most often the present tense.
The incidents she relates receive the simplest descriptive
narration, a lineal development with no flash backs or
subtle time schemes. In these beginning years of the
twentieth century, the two important novelists of Colette's generation, Proust and Gide, were in search of
new forms for the novel. Colette, and in this respect she
was not to change, was concerned mainly with the direct
telling of a story. There is nothing that is complicated
or involved in the structure of the *Claudine* novels. They
follow the various experiences of Claudine from the age
of fifteen to the age of thirty, from her school days to
the death of her husband, Renaud. The outer events of
Claudine's life reflect those of Colette's. Claudine's happy
country adolescence, her early marriage and the artistic-
Bohemian surroundings in which it placed her, her
eventual retreat to the country, are obvious borrowings
from Colette's own life.

However, there are in these novels a few important
departures from the facts of Colette's life. If Renaud,
Claudine's seducer and her husband, bears a certain
moral resemblance to Monsieur Willy, the aging, tender
Renaud of *La Retraite sentimentale*, who has abandoned
all extramarital pursuits, and the dying, ideal Renaud
of the same novel are very far indeed from Colette's first
husband. Claudine's father, an absent-minded entomol-

ogist with an amazing repertory of smutty songs, so different from Colette's own father as portrayed in "Le
Capitaine," represents another significant deviation from
the "real." Unlike Colette, Claudine is an only child.
But the most striking and revealing discrepancy between
Colette's own life and the life of her character, Claudine,
is the absence of a mother, the absence of Sido. Claudine's family is reduced to a father, a housemaid, Mélie,
and a cat, Fanchette. It is not too difficult to imagine
why Colette excluded from these novels Sido, the person
she most loved. Sido was still alive in the opening years
of the twentieth century, and Colette quite obviously did
not wish to associate her mother with the scandalous
antics of her other characters. It was not until 1922, ten
years after Sido's death, that Colette began to write
about her mother, to use her as the major figure in many
of her works.

Although the narrator, Claudine, changes in the
course of the five novels, she remains a young girl or a
young woman of a certain recognizable type, the first in
the long series of Colette's feminine creations. Sensitive,
precocious, egotistical, impertinent, sensual, all these adjectives characterize the different Claudines, though one
or another seems particularly applicable to Colette's
heroine at different periods of her life. However, like
Colette herself and like all Colette's female characters,
Claudine, despite her apparent wildness and amorality,
frequently and rather surprisingly reminds us that she
is, at heart, a very simple bourgeoise.

In the beginning pages of *Claudine à l'Ecole*, Claudine, "the beautiful savage," introduces herself to the
reader. She is a native of the village of Montigny, a

literary transposition of Saint-Sauveur-en-Puisaye, and a lover of the woods around the town. Claudine speaks of these woods and their odors with special affection because she is fifteen, because she is to enter her last year at school and because she feels that she is changing. She has to wear long skirts, she is becoming a woman and she may soon have to leave the beloved woods, symbol of her childhood and her liberty. This first novel opens with one of the most important themes of Colette's entire literary production, the always exuberant evocation of a childhood spent in a small village, the joy of being alone "in" nature, of looking, of smelling.

The little, old school of Montigny, "this unique, improbable and delicious school," [7] is the focal point of *Claudine à l'Ecole*. School is a place where Claudine is never bored, where intrigues are created and flourish. Claudine's classmates, the big Anaïs, the Jaubert sisters, Marie Belhomme and Luce, the sister of the young instructress, Aimée Lanthenay, are the daughters of peasants, policemen and workers. Although they are adolescents like Claudine, she treats them with a superior disdain. They, too, are troubled by the eternal adolescent drama of the often violent awakening and demands of the senses, the desire to love and to be loved, the uncertainty that accompanies inexperience. They are, in general, less distant than Claudine, less restrained in the display of their sentiments. Luce openly shows her affection for Claudine, as Anaïs openly shows her affection for the boys, whereas Claudine, although moved by the feline beauty of Luce and her sister, Aimée, confines most of her feelings to her journal. There is in Claudine a strong sensual drive, but there is also an adolescent love of purity, a certain withdrawal and disgust in the face of physical love.

The novel, which follows the course of the school year, from autumn to summer, contains two main lines of development. One is centered on the jealous love of the red-headed directress, Mademoiselle Sergent, for the young instructress, Mademoiselle Lanthenay. The latter accepts this love, but is also willing to accept the attentions of one of the young male instructors at the adjacent boys' school. The complications are infinite, particularly since Mademoiselle Sergent is also the mistress of Monsieur Dutertre, a local politician and Don Juan. Jealous and repelled by what she sees and overhears [8] of the caresses and whisperings of the two women, Claudine becomes a veritable demon in the classroom.

The second, less intense but still dramatic, line of development is centered on the classroom and the incidents and interruptions caused by Claudine in her desire to disrupt, to destroy, to be recognized, and culminates in the very amusing account of how Claudine and her classmates pass their final examinations. The novel ends with a tremendous explosion at the end of the school year. A fête for which the entire village prepares, and in which the schoolchildren participate, is given in honor of the local deputy. In the evening, a ball is held at the schoolhouse. Mademoiselle Sergent and Monsieur Dutertre are discovered in a most compromising situation by the former's mother, who screams the news to the assembled crowd. Thus, on a note of scandal, Claudine's last year of school comes to a close.

The first of the five novels of the *Claudine* series is by far the most successful. Although Colette was coerced by

Monsieur Willy into writing all but the last of these novels, the first *Claudine* has a freshness and a completeness that are lacking in the others. The reason for this is quite simple. Colette wrote the original version of *Claudine à l'Ecole* by herself.[9] Later, Monsieur Willy made changes and additions and suggested the kinds of incidents and characters he wanted in the other novels of the series. And Colette very obligingly followed all the directions. But when she wrote *Claudine à l'Ecole* she had not, as yet, come under the literary tutelage of her husband. She had been told to write, not how to write, and despite Willy's tamperings the novel remains very definitely Colette's.

Colette was able to deal with adolescent love and desire against the background of a small village, its "characters," its intrigues, its rituals and its fêtes, a rural setting which she knew well. Were it not for her ability to handle ambiguous relationships in a rather detached way, treating the feelings of Mademoiselle Sergent, Aimée, Luce and Claudine, not as monstrous or perverted, but as possible and humorous manifestations of human nature, the novel would have been little more than a rather scandalous story about adolescents which adolescents should not read.

The point of view of a fifteen-year-old Claudine both allows Colette to maintain a certain freedom and obliges her to remain within certain bounds. *Claudine à l'Ecole*, introduces the reader to the world of physical love through the emotions of a young girl who, although sensual and curious, is herself completely inexperienced. Colette, from the very beginning of her literary career, shows mastery in the art of translating the sensations of those who stand on the threshold of love. When, however, in the succeeding novels of the series, under the precise guidance of Monsieur Willy, Colette attempts to describe the actual love-making of a group of amoral, flat characters, she loses this mastery, and the reader is taken from the realm of light literature into that of curious anecdotes. Colette was, at this period, incapable of transposing into fiction the machinations of a certain sophisticated Paris set, nor was she able to create convincing characters on the basis of Willy's suggestions. Indeed, Colette was never to become a great creator of characters. She was able to transpose real people into fictional creations, but only with great difficulty could she invent fictional characters and make them real.

Claudine à Paris and *Claudine en Ménage* are closer to scandal sheets than to light novels. Claudine and her father have moved to Paris, and Claudine, after an illness, resumes the writing of her journal. She dislikes Paris, the closed apartment of the rue Jacob, and she dreams of Montigny and her beloved woods. Claudine is surrounded almost immediately by a strange set of characters, all of whom are obsessed by physical desires. She finds herself in a world in which the force of physical attraction dominates all human activities, a world in which people seem to do nothing but make love or talk of making love.

There is a mixture of curiosity, dislike and irony in Claudine's depiction of these characters, as, by the use of exaggerated realism, she describes both a very particular Paris milieu at the turn of the century and what is, apparently, Colette's own reaction to it. Marcel, the too handsome young man whom Claudine meets at her aunt's, not content with being a rabid homosexual, exhibits a morbid curiosity about Claudine's private life; Luce, whom Claudine accidentally meets in Paris, is being kept by her pudgy middle-aged uncle; Mélie, the housekeeper, has but one ambition, which is to bring together all the single people she can find; Fanchette, the cat, is pregnant—in short, everyone is having or has had a strong dose of physical love. And this hothouse atmosphere, reminiscent of the school at Montigny, is intensified by the songs of Claudine's father, which become more and more obscene.

Claudine herself succumbs very easily, succumbs to the charms of Marcel's forty-year-old father, Renaud, a handsome, dissipated Don Juan. At the moment when Claudine has decided to become his mistress, they are married, a rather amusing turn of events which Colette also uses in *Gigi*. But this marriage does not subdue all of Claudine's fires, and in *Claudine en Ménage* the reader is confronted with the contrived triangle, Claudine-Renaud-Rézi.[10] Always sensitive to extreme feminine charm, Claudine, with her husband's connivance, has a passionate love affair with Rézi . . . but then, so does Renaud. Claudine flees to Montigny, to her beloved woods, to escape from Renaud's betrayal. But love conquers all, and she writes to him; he comes to her.

This happy ending of *Claudine en Ménage*, so different from the course that the marital relations between Colette and Willy were to take, marks a turning point in the novels of the *Claudine* series. Complicated love affairs continue to blossom, but Claudine and Renaud are spectators rather than participants. They become the ideal, contented couple; they observe the antics of their friends.

The fourth novel, *Claudine s'en va*, brings a welcome variation. The center of attention has shifted, and Claudine is no longer the narrator. The book is the journal of one of Claudine's friends, Annie. Colette, here, has really synthesized two novels: one which anticipates her later and more complex works, another which merely continues to deal with the world of physical attractions and sexual play of the two preceding novels. The "first" novel, which eventually loses itself in the confusion of the "second," is the study of Annie's awakening to life.

Annie begins to keep a journal because, for the first time since her marriage to Alain, she is alone. Accustomed to obeying her husband, to receiving and executing his orders, Annie is completely lost when Alain leaves Paris to collect an inheritance in Buenos Aires. He has given her a written schedule of things to do, but Annie, who never did anything by herself, is only partially helped by this pattern on paper. Gradually, as she writes in her journal and sees people through her own eyes, she gains in lucidity. She discovers, not only that her rigid, bourgeois husband has been unfaithful, but that she, Annie, although tied to Alain by habit and ignorance, heartily dislikes him. However, Colette, or perhaps Willy, does not allow this part of the novel to occupy the foreground. Whether in Paris or at the Wagner festival in Bayreuth, Annie is inevitably involved with a strange group. The reconciled ménage of Claudine and Renaud, the unhappy ménage of Marthe and Léon, Annie's sister and novelist brother-in-law, the alcoholic music critic Maugis, these people and others turn in their own little orbits around Annie. Annie's share in the story is finally submerged in a flood of liaisons, of small talk and of much sentimental advice from Claudine.

Although Annie is the major character in this novel, it is still Claudine whose name appears in the title. Annie, who in the course of the story discovers the absurdity and falseness of her past life, sets out by herself to seek for that love which Claudine has already found. Claudine and Renaud leave Paris, in order to live in peace and harmony in the village of Montigny.

In the last volume of the *Claudine* series, *La Retraite sentimentale* (1907), Claudine is again the narrator. Five years have passed since the end of *Claudine s'en va*, and Claudine is living with Annie in the latter's country house, *Casamène*.[11] Renaud is in the hospital, and Claudine, completely in love with her husband, is patiently awaiting his return. The opening pages of the novel describe the everyday life of Claudine: the letters from Renaud, the garden, the walks she takes with Toby-Chien, her memories of Montigny and her talks with Annie. In the five years which have elapsed, Annie has become a confirmed nymphomaniac, and her brief love affairs, which she relates in detail to Claudine, seem to have no other raison d'être than to shock and to entice the avid reader.

Marcel, Renaud's son and Claudine's stepson, sick and in debt, comes to *Casamène*, and Claudine has nothing better to do than to arrange a sordid scene between her ardently homosexual stepson and Annie, so amorous of any young masculine flesh. Renaud returns from the hospital an old and sick man and dies shortly after his return. Annie, unable to obtain any moral benefits from a prolonged contact with nature, leaves to seek new adventures. Claudine remains alone at *Casamène* with her animals and the memory of her love. Eighteen months after Renaud's death, Annie, Maugis, Marthe and Léon come to *Casamène* to visit Claudine. They are shocked by her aloofness to them and by her inner calm. Claudine, living in the country, surrounded by her animals and her memories, has, at last, found peace.

This novel is redeemed by the last pages, in which Claudine learns how to live and to accept both what is inevitable in life, death, and what make the beauty of life, memories and nature. It is redeemed also by the scenes in which Claudine walks in the woods and talks with Toby-Chien, scenes which echo those of the *Dialogues de Bêtes* written three years before.[12] In the rest of the novel, it is quite obvious that Colette has been carried away into a superficial exploration of the world of physical desires. When writing *La Retraite sentimentale*, Colette was no longer under the supervision of Monsieur Willy, she was no longer wearing the mask; but she had been strongly marked by it. In the stories Annie tells of her successive brief encounters, and in the pathetic scene between Marcel and Annie, Colette has fallen into the trap of the off-color story, the pornographic anecdote. But this book nevertheless signalizes a definite return, on Colette's part, to her own particular world and values. The retreat to nature as the necessary source of moral courage receives its first full treatment at the end of *La Retraite sentimentale*, which echoes and amplifies the opening pages of *Claudine à l'Ecole*. Claudine's cyclical journey has carried her from a natural state of purity and freedom to a world which destroys this original bliss and back again to nature, where a delicate equilibrium between Claudine and her past life is finally achieved. This equilibrium has its sources in Claudine's stoical acceptance of the vicissitudes of human life and in her epicurean joy in the always wondrous natural world.

It is no mere coincidence that Colette, at the end of *La Retraite sentimentale*, published one year after her divorce from Willy, rejects the confused Paris crowd and brings Claudine back to the country, to a renewed contact with her childhood, with woods, animals and flowers. The death of Renaud, the distance maintained by Claudine during the condolence call paid by her former friends, are a kind of symbolic projection of Colette's new state of mind. She, too, has given up the Paris world which, as a human being, she dislikes, with which, as a novelist, she feels incompetent to deal. Later Colette is to come back to the private world which Monsieur Willy revealed to her, the world of physical love. "All my novels which followed are, however, minute analyses of love, and I have not tired of it. But I began to put love in novels and to be pleased with what I was doing only when I had regained esteem for love—and for myself." [13]

It is in the novel *La Vagabonde* (1911) that Colette begins again to write of love. The emphasis here is no longer on the physical act alone, but on the moral and psychological as well as the physical complications of a love relationship. In all the novels in which Colette writes of love, from *La Vagabonde* to *Gigi*, there is an aura of purity which is completely lacking in the *Claudine* series, certain pages in *Claudine à l'Ecole* and in *La Retraite sentimentale* excepted.

Minne and *Les égarements de Minne*, published respectively in 1904 and 1905 and combined in 1909 under the title *L'Ingénue libertine*, contain the same artistic successes and failures as the novels of the *Claudine* series. Once again, the failures can be attributed, in large part, to Monsieur Willy and to Colette's mask. Colette wrote *Minne* because she wanted to write a short story of her own inspiration to which she could sign her own name. However, Willy not only affixed his signature to the story but, delighted with its success, demanded a sequel. And *Minne*, which began as the charming tale of a child's fantasies and dreams, became, in *Les égarements de Minne*, a series of bedroom adventures only too reminiscent of *Claudine à Paris* and *Claudine en Ménage*.

When she joined the two stories into one novel, Colette made certain significant omissions. Aside from cutting out extraneous words and passages, as she always tended to do in rewriting, Colette, this time, did away with most of the homosexual puns and references which Willy, undoubtedly, had induced her to use most generously in the original versions. These included, in *Minne*, references to an English school friend who kissed Minne and, in *Les égarements de Minne*, Maugis's rather raw comments on Irène Chaulieu's Sapphism. Despite this rewriting, Colette was dissatisfied.

> . . . I had then to write *Les égarements de Minne,*
> which I could never consider a good novel.
> Was it better when it later become my property, when
> I welded it, shortened, unburdened, to *Minne*, in order to

make one volume under the title: *L'Ingénue libertine*? I would like to think so, but I fear that even this definitive edition will not succeed in giving me certitude, nor in completely reconciling me with the first aspects of my career as novelist.[14]

The original *Minne*, like parts of *Claudine à l'Ecole* and the last pages of *La Retraite sentimentale*, owes its success to the fact that Colette began writing without Willy's intervention. In contrast to the *Claudine* novels, the story is told in the third person and there is no relation between the facts of Colette's life and those of her heroine's. A beautiful, blond adolescent of fourteen, Minne lives more in the world of fantasy than in the world of reality. In a Paris newspaper, in a column entitled "Paris la Nuit," she reads of the nightly adventures of a band of gangsters and assassins whose leader is Le Frisé. Minne has adopted this underground world as her own, and Le Frisé has become her ideal. She loves him and wants to be his woman and, in the absence of Casque de Cuivre, the new Queen of the gang. Minne is not allowed to live only in this world of adolescent fantasies. There is Maman, a "young widow, timid and domestic," there is Minne's sickly Uncle Paul, and there is her eighteen-year-old cousin, Antoine, who adores her. But Antoine, with his sudden desires, his inexperienced fumblings and his pimples, can hardly compete with the qualities Minne has attributed to Le Frisé.

The story ends with the collapse of Minne's invented world. Convinced that Le Frisé is waiting for her, Minne steals out of her house at night. After a series of nightmarish street encounters, however, she returns home, obliged to recognize that the world she has created does not exist. Successfully intertwined with the story of the creation and dissolution of Minne's inner world is that of Antoine's awkward, adolescent love. The delicacy with which Colette treats the moment when a young boy moves from friendship to an awareness of desire and love announces the fuller treatment of this theme in *Le Blé en herbe* (1923). The differences between Antoine and Claudine's stepson, Marcel, are glaringly apparent. Antoine is first in the series of Colette's sensitive adolescent boys, a series that includes Chéri in *Chéri* (1928), Phil in *Le Blé en herbe*, Jean Farou in *La Seconde* (1929) and Toni in *Julie de Carneilhan* (1941).

Minne, Antoine and the first Claudine, all belong to the same family. Minne meets the first signs of physical desire by escaping into a world of fantasy; Claudine meets them with a desire to love, to caress men and women, animals and plants; Antoine, more realistically, centers his desires on one real and attainable object. Antoine, unlike Minne and Claudine, is fortunate in having his desire and his love coincide.

"I am going to sleep with Minne." [15] This opening sentence sets the tone and indicates the subject of *Les égarements de Minne*, now the second part of *L'Ingénue libertine*. Minne is Antoine's wife. Minne is not happy. In the two years of her marriage, she has never known the pleasures of physical love, an insufficiency which she is the only one of Colette's characters ever to have experienced. Too good, too kind, Antoine is so far removed from Minne's earlier idol, Le Frisé, that she remains cold and unfeeling in her husband's arms. And so Minne sets out to "find" physical pleasure. But not the young and amorous Baron Couderc, whose unrequited love for

Minne ends in an unsuccessful and rather ridiculous suicide attempt, not Maugis, who understands her, not any of the men to whom she gives herself, is able to lead Minne into this closed and unknown world.

Unlike most of Colette's novels (another exception is *Gigi*), *L'Ingénue libertine* ends happily. Antoine, although deeply wounded by his wife's infidelities, loves Minne so much that he is willing to accept everything for the sake of Minne's happiness. Minne is, for the first time, touched by the generosity of Antoine's love. And one night at Monte Carlo, by way of recognition for her husband's liberality, she invites him to sleep with her. Miracle of miracles, Minne finds with her husband that which she has been searching for elsewhere. This is one of the rare occasions in a Colette novel when, because they are able to give something more than their bodies, a man and a woman find happiness in love. Unfortunately, the ending is too sentimental, too abrupt, to be very convincing.

# VIII

Renée and the End of Renée

The illusion of freedom is as good as free-dom.[1]

The six years that Colette spent "going from one music hall to another music hall, from a mime friend to an acrobat friend, from a chanteuse friend to a danseuse friend,"[2] were to furnish the décor for one novel, *La Vagabonde* (1911), and for a series of fictionalized reminiscences, *L'Envers du Music-Hall* (1913), the first fictional works in France that gave a true image of music-hall life. Unlike most of Colette's novels, *La Vagabonde* was written during the period it describes. Because of this fact, *La Vagabonde* is the most lyrical, the most intensely personal of the novels, and Renée Néré, the first-person heroine, the least fictional of Colette's fictional creations. *L'Entrave*, published in 1913, is a sequel to *La Vagabonde*. Although in *L'Entrave* the music hall no longer supplies the décor, the two novels bear a striking similarity in structure. There are three principal characters involved in each case and their relationship to each other is the same: Renée, her lover, Maxime, and the enigmatic Hammond in *La Vagabonde*; Renée, her lover, Jean, and the enigmatic Masseau in *L'Entrave*. These two novels might well be called *Renée* and *The End of Renée*; as with *Chéri* and *La fin de Chéri*, the first novel proposes a temporary solution to the drama, a solution which the end of the second novel proves inadequate.

In certain respects, Renée is Claudine grown older, a Claudine who would have married Maugis rather than Renaud. That Renée and Claudine share the same country childhood and adolescence is clear from the few remarks that Renée makes about her youth, but this happy childhood plays no part in the novels. Its mention is significant only insofar as it establishes a link between Renée, Claudine and, of course, Colette. Like Claudine, Renée writes, although Claudine's writing is confined to her journal, whereas Renée has published four books. They are both passionately interested in themselves, and just as passionately aroused by a passing cat, a beautiful landscape. Claudine's return to the country and to peace in *La Retraite sentimentale* is, in essence, a gesture similar to Renée's wholehearted giving of herself to her lover at the end of *L'Entrave*. In both instances, the ending marks a split between the lives of the characters and the life of their creator.

Almost all the other facts of Renée's life have their counterpart in facts of Colette's own life: an overwhelming first love which resulted in a disastrous marriage and a brutal awakening to certain aspects of life and suffering—particularly to the all-consuming power of

jealousy; a divorce which led both to a solitary existence
and to the career of music-hall mime; [3] a love affair
which ended, at least for Colette, and it may be assumed
for Renée also, in marriage. The important difference
between Renée and her creator is that during this period
Colette never ceased to write, she never retired from an
active working life as did the Renée of *L'Entrave*. In this
sense, it might be said that Renée represents one of Colette's temptations—the temptation to "do" nothing, to
be completely possessed by love. To this temptation Colette never succumbed, perhaps because she never found
a man who could so completely possess her, more possibly because she could never stop writing.

The problem posed and resolved in these two novels
is the very general problem of how to live a life. The
terms in which it is posed are limited, as always in Colette's novels, to a particular kind of situation and a particular kind of woman. The opening pages of *La Vagabonde* establish what is given in the situation. Renée
Néré is thirty-three years old. She was married to a
famous portrait painter, Adolph Taillandy; she has divorced him and has become a music-hall mime in order
to earn her living. But the music hall, for Renée as for
Colette, is more than a means of livelihood. It is a way
of life admirably suited to a woman who wishes to maintain "the illusion of freedom." The demands of the music
hall are many, and Renée does not conceal any of the
details: constant rehearsals, sordid dressing rooms, fa-
tiguing tours, cheap hotels, constant physical discomfort
and difficult audiences. Music-hall life imposes its own
particular routines and restrictions. Renée is a *vagabonde* because she belongs to a music-hall troupe; she is

forced to wander, to abandon the green glen she spies from the window of a moving train, the friends and lovers with whom, after chance and always brief encounters, she may wish to linger. But in a deeper sense, Renée partakes of the advantages of vagabondage without having to face any of its practical difficulties. She moves because she has to move; there is little personal choice involved. Her vagabondage is restricted and determined by the exigencies of her métier.

In her contacts with the other vagabonds, Renée is able to maintain that distance which she deems so necessary to personal survival. She admires in her companions their pride, which is a reflection of her own, their discreet poverty and above all their silence—their refusal to speak of their private lives. And yet Renée is quite obviously not one of them. Her social background, her literary achievements and also her deep sense of superiority mark the gap between Renée and the others. They remain, for her, "rudimentary creatures," who "hardly think at all." Frightened of human contacts, particularly of men and of love, surrounded by her silent cohorts, Renée is a lonely woman holding tenaciously to her personal liberty, to her organized life of vagabondage. From her "respectable" past, two forces continue to exert their influence over her present: her unhappy first marriage and her writing. These abandoned positions of wife and writer color both Renée's story and the way in which it is told. If the problem of love originated in Renée's unfortunate marital experiences, which left her with the fear that a second love might resemble the first, her lengthy monologue owes its special quality to Renée's ability to perceive and to transform her perceptions into words. The credibility of the novel is due, in great part, to the fact that Renée has been a writer.

Within this particular situation, the general problem of how to live a life is reduced to the following: Can a woman both love and remain free, and is there any more to love than the voluptuous joys of the body? *La Vagabonde* moves from Renée's initial "no" to the first part of this problem to a timid "yes" and then to a final "no." The response to the second part of the problem follows a different curve: an initial "no" to a final "yes." *L'Entrave* ends with the same answers. The Renée of the last pages of *L'Entrave* has made the choice between liberty and love, and the reader is led to believe, by a false analogy between the particular and the general, that for a woman it is the only possible choice, that only a man can be a vagabond, that a woman is never free because she cannot live without a man. Yet it is obvious that Colette is not proposing a sociological or psychological solution to the female problem, although it would not be far-fetched to say that in *La Vagabonde* she is dealing in very concrete terms with one of the twentieth century's most written-about questions—marriage versus a career. It would be an error, nonetheless, to consider the end of *L'Entrave* as any more than the resolution of the particular dilemma of Renée Néré, and of women like Renée Néré. In *La Vagabonde*, when Renée is a music-hall mime, a woman with a career, she can oppose to the world of security offered her by Maxime her own world of rehearsals and tours, her mute friendships with the members of her troupe and, last but not least, the ever-present desire to write. Renée's apparent acquiescence to Maxime's proposal of marriage at the end of the second

part of *La Vagabonde* is followed by what is supposed to
be her last tour. It is during this tour that Renée's relation to Maxime is "modified." [4] Renée's conscious awareness of this "modification" occurs after she has contemplated, alone, the beauty of the coast and sea at Sète [5] in
the south of France.

> Yes, [I have] forgotten him, as if I had never known his
> glance or the caress of his mouth, forgotten him as if there
> were no more imperious need in my life than to look for
> words, for words to describe how yellow the sun is and
> how blue the sea and how brilliant the salt in fringes of
> white jet. Yes, forgotten him as if the only urgent thing in
> the world were my desire to possess through my eyes the
> marvels of the earth. [6]

This theme of *"Regarde"* of the all-important relation
between the individual and the world, between the
writer and the world, a relation which admits of no outside interference or orientation, is intensified in one of
Renée's final outbursts. "But you counted without my
beggar-woman's pride: I refuse to see the most beautiful
countries of the world microscopically reflected in the
amorous mirror of your eyes." [7] Renée the perceiver,
Renée the writer must needs be alone, must refuse any
intrusion between herself and "the most beautiful countries of the world."

In *L'Entrave*, the situation is very different. Renée is
a retired mime; she lives in a hotel in Nice; she does
nothing. She no longer refers to herself as an ex-writer
or as a potential writer. She can oppose to the world of
love offered her by Jean no world of her own. And so it
may be said that Renée's final acceptance of Jean is the

only possibility open to her in her given situation—it is indeed a last resort.

There are two very curious characters in these novels, characters who are, in great part, responsible for Renée's "last resort" choice. Hammond, in *La Vagabonde*, is an old friend of Renée, the only person with whom she will discuss her past, for Hammond, too, had an unhappy first marriage. And it is Hammond who eases Renée into Maxime's arms. It is Hammond, the old, heartbroken man, who almost convinces Renée that love is still possible. In *L'Entrave*, Hammond, dead, is replaced by Masseau, the opium-smoking friend of Renée's potential lover, Jean. And it is Masseau who acts as a kind of "providence," who creates the "no-exit" situations, who leads Renée and Jean to each other.

Both Hammond and Masseau are somewhat fantastic creatures, birdlike, sexless men, who talk incessantly. And although Hammond fails in his desire to keep Renée and Maxime together, it is Masseau whose surprisingly homespun philosophy triumphs in *L'Entrave*. This cynical, vice-ridden old man still believes in love, in the possibility of love between two "ordinary people." What Masseau tells Renée in his rather sentimental discourse on love is that she can retain Jean only by giving all of herself to him, and that she is capable of doing this because she is an "ordinary" woman, a woman who has "no genius." A great deal of Renée's monologue, both in *La Vagabonde* and in *L'Entrave*, has been devoted to assuring the reader and herself that she is no ordinary woman, that she does, indeed, have a kind of genius. "It is only in pain that a woman is capable of rising above mediocrity," [8] is one of Renée's general statements about the female species, a statement which both situates Renée biologically and affirms her superiority. Her final yielding to Masseau's advice, and thus to Jean, is an explicit renunciation of this superiority and an explicit avowal of the validity of another very general and beautifully expressed thought: "Voluptuousness occupies, in the limitless desert of love, an ardent and very small place." [9] And indeed if Renée is to accept Jean, what she must reject is the penetrating scrutiny she has always bestowed both on herself and on others, this keen appraisal which tends to reduce people, and particularly men, to objects.

In reading *La Vagabonde* and *L'Entrave*, one is often embarrassed, without quite knowing why. The reader has the feeling that he shouldn't be reading, that he has been placed in a position of uncomfortable intimacy. This embarrassment does not have its source in any detailed descriptions of love-making, for Colette never gives the details directly, but rather in Renée's unbelievable awareness and sensitivity to herself, her desire and the desire of her partner. Renée's harping on her age, on her wrinkles, on the dangers for a thirty-six-year-old woman of bursting into tears, of being seen in the early morning light, are realistic touches that add to the discomfort. One is not used to being given so concrete a portrayal of the trifling annoyances that beset a woman. Renée's awareness makes both of Maxime's and later of Jean's desire, an object, and as an object it becomes somewhat repulsive. At one point in *L'Entrave*, Jean accuses Renée of "employing" him, rather than loving him, and this, of course, is Renée's flaw as a woman, though not as a writer. Just as Renée gives her body to

Jean, refusing him, until the end, everything else, so
Renée expects of Jean only that he give his body and
tends to see him only as a body. So reduced, he appears a
flat, weak character. Renée's love-talk with Jean is limited to a few remarks on his physical beauty, on the "rapport" which exists between their two bodies.

But Renée must not be judged in the light of conventional morality. If she sees Jean and his desire as objects,
if she employs Jean as a means to pleasure, it is in part
out of a very sane fear of mistaking that thing called
"love" for any more than what it really is. Renée knows
that the pleasure derived from love-making is the greatest of pleasures. She knows, too, that this pleasure is only
temporary peace, a temporary communication. She questions whether there is any other possible form of communication between two lovers. And if the very "moral"
conclusion of *L'Entrave*, a conclusion that makes of the
novel a kind of thesis novel, is not quite satisfying, it is
because Renée's hesitancy in accepting a more traditional definition of love seems somehow more courageous, more lucid, than her final plunge, in which her
tone becomes that of a person newly converted, a pe-
dantic, irritating tone. Or is it that here creator and
character have come into conflict? Was Colette so close
to Renée that when she tried to give Renée a solution of
her own, the portrait somehow fell apart? Is not the
Renée of *La Vagabonde* who asks, "Are you sure that
happiness is enough for me henceforward?" [10] the convincing Renée, the Colette-Renée, and the Renée who
moves toward her conventional happiness less convincing because her creator is so little convinced?

 IX

Mitsou and Gigi

*"This child disheartens me. . . . She comes
from another planet."* [1]

The year 1919–1920 marks a new and important development in Colette's work. Until this date Colette, almost exclusively, had used a first-person narrator in her
writings. With the publication of *Mitsou*, in 1919, the
barely disguised confessions which characterize her novels from the *Claudines* to *L'Entrave* are apparently
abandoned.

In the years immediately preceding the first World
War, Colette began her career as a journalist. Although
many of her articles are written in a very imaginative,
impressionistic style, and although the first-person narrator often dominates them, newspaper writing, both of
articles and serialized stories, forced Colette to a degree
of objectivity and economy which her writings had
hitherto lacked. This perhaps partially explains the fact
that *Mitsou*, the first short novel she wrote after her

initial years as a journalist, and all the novels which were written after *Mitsou* are more objective, more condensed, than her early writings.

The change from a first-person to a third-person narrator was to influence Colette's style and the form her novels took, rather than the novels' characterizations. Indeed, the word "novel" hardly applies to Colette's fictional writings from *Mitsou* to *Gigi*, particularly if one considers a novel to be a work of a certain length. The longest novel of this period, *La Seconde*, has only one hundred and fifty pages. However, since Colette herself referred to these works as novels, rather than novelettes or long short stories, the present study will employ the same term.

As these novels become progressively shorter, they tend also to be more and more devoid of any description which does not bear directly on the action. The landscapes of which Colette was so fond disappear almost completely. The long, lyrical passages so frequent in the early novels are totally absent. Colette concentrates on dialogue, on the unspoken thoughts of her characters and on descriptions of their gestures, their facial expressions, their physical and their mental states. The constraint imposed on Colette by her effort to conceive and organize a sequence of events which do not necessarily stem directly from her own experience is reflected in a change in her prose; it becomes less verbose, more disciplined, a vehicle both for irony and humor.

Mitsou and *Gigi* were written in time of war, *Mitsou* toward the end of the first World War and *Gigi* toward the end of the second. The twenty-five years that separate the two novels enable us to see some of the changes that took place in Colette's approach to the craft of fiction.

The time at which the novel was written and the time depicted in it coincide in *Mitsou*. Although *Mitsou* can hardly be considered a "war" story, the war plays a part in creating the atmosphere and situations of the novel: the excitement engendered in Mitsou's music-hall colleague, Petite Chose, by the presence of so many uniformed young men, the conditions under which Mitsou meets her "blue" lieutenant, the fact that they have only one night together, the importance of their correspondence. But the war, like the music hall, is merely the background for the main theme, which is, as Colette herself has defined it in the subtitle, "How intelligence comes to young girls."

Gigi was written when Colette was turning seventy; it is her last work of fiction and her adieu to a bygone age. The source of this short novel was an anecdote related to Colette in 1926. The most significant change made by Colette in her transformation of the anecdote into fiction was a time change. The events related in 1926 had taken place in 1918; the action of *Gigi* takes place in 1899, at the time when Colette, guided by Willy, had come to know the demimondaine world. It is the period of the early *Claudines*; Colette has returned to her point of departure.

In writing *Gigi*, Colette reduced to a minimum the necessity of inventing and imagining. For the characters given in the anecdote, Colette easily found models from her own fictional world and from her past acquaintance. That this past should have remained so vivid is proof of the influence it exerted on Colette and its fusion in her mind with the even more remote past of her childhood. Despite her age, her arthritis and her concern for her husband's safety, Colette was able to evoke this past as if it were present. The distance between Colette and her characters is considerably smaller in *Gigi* than in *Mitsou*, and this is an important factor in the superiority of *Gigi*.

Mitsou is Colette's only experimental novel. It is obviously an attempt at integrating into one novel certain techniques which Colette had already used in *Les Dialogues de Bêtes* and in *La Vagabonde*. *Mitsou* is a half-dramatic, half-epistolary novel. The alternation of stage settings and dialogue with letters allows Colette to describe quickly and to present humorously Mitsou and her world and also to show the changes that occur in Mitsou and her "blue" lieutenant through their correspondence. Thus the characters are presented objectively, as the author sees them and as they speak, and subjectively, as they see and understand themselves. The subjective, first-person presentation is much less successful than the objective. Colette herself was undoubtedly aware of this, since *Mitsou* is the last of her novels in which she includes a subjective presentation of character.

Gigi is a very simply narrated story in which, as always in Colette's fiction, the largest share of the writing is given over to dialogue. The double surprise ending, Gigi's acceptance of Gaston's proposal on his terms and Gaston's final acceptance of Gigi on very different terms, seems to be an anomaly in Colette's usual presentation of the game of love. But the happy, Cinderella ending was in the anecdote and Colette faithfully kept to her source.

The names "Mitsou" and "Gigi" evoke a certain milieu and a certain kind of snub-nosed young girl or woman. Mitsou and Gigi are lucid and romantic, simple and proud. They share with the other "Colette-Claudines" uncanny intuition and common sense, coupled with great naïveté and piquant beauty. The adjectives that best fit them, "cute," "pretty" and "nice," have, in the past years, been so abused as to be almost useless. They are, however, admirably suited to a general description of Colette's young ladies.

Because of their sincerity and their innate refusal to accept conventional or unconventional norms of behavior, Mitsou and Gigi are rather amusing characters. A rich source of humor, particularly for the American and British reader, is that neither Mitsou nor Gigi does what is expected of her. Neither of them conforms to preconceived and often literary notions of how a show girl and the offspring of an unwed mother should act. Both emerge morally untainted from a demimondaine environment, and both are saved, or rather save themselves, by love.

Mitsou, at twenty-four, is a music-hall dancer at the Empyrée theater in Paris. The established mistress of an elderly "respectable man," Mitsou has never been in love until she accidentally meets the "blue" lieutenant. Her life is the routine, dull life of which Renée speaks in *La Vagabonde*. Like Renée, like Colette herself, Mitsou, the music-hall star, has more good will than talent; her success is due to her personal appeal rather than to her art. Indeed, in all she does, Mitsou is disarmingly artless. On stage and off, she is very simply and irreducibly Mitsou. Hence her charm.

Gigi, at fifteen, looks "like Robin Hood, like a stiff angel, like a boy in skirts, she seldom resembled a young girl." [2] Although Gigi is definitely female, she is unselfconsciously female, she is still at an ambiguous, equivocal age and, like so many of Colette's adolescents, combines the physical graces of both sexes. The comparisons chosen by Colette to describe Gigi acquire an added force by the very fact that they are the only images in the novel which refer to a world not limited to the demimonde. Thus, from the beginning, Colette is attempting to portray Gigi as a general type of adolescent as well as a product of a very particular social group.

The daughter of an unimportant singer at the Opéra-Comique, the granddaughter and grandniece of two retired courtesans, Gigi is receiving from her exclusively female entourage the training necessary for her future career as the mistress of wealthy men. Gigi is taught by her grandmother, Madame Alvarez, to keep her knees close to each other when she is seated, to keep her legs together when she is standing. She is told not to wear stays because they spoil the figure, not to get to know the fathers of her school friends. She is taught by her great-aunt Alicia how to select cigars, how to distinguish between precious stones, how to eat lobster, American style. Aside from her restricted contacts with her school friends, Gigi's relation to the world outside the family is limited to the mundane gossip in the newspaper *Gil Blas*—real news referring to real people, like Polaire and Liane de Pougy—and the erratic visits of Gaston Lachaille, the bored and very wealthy son of one of Madame Alvarez's former lovers.

These highly readable, unpretentious stories contain a wealth of subtle details and moral implications which become particularly significant when seen in relation to the rest of Colette's writing. By themselves, they are more or less delightful, slice-of-life, period tales. As parts of a whole, they are chapters illustrating varied aspects and styles of the game of love.

Both *Mitsou* and *Gigi* are concerned with the problem of education. For Mitsou, the education is accomplished through love, and as the progress in style in Mitsou's letters over an eight-month period shows, it is a very rapid education, a very painful but tangible gain in awareness. Whether or not Mitsou will ever win back her disillusioned "blue" lieutenant she is, in any case, victorious, because she has had the experience of love, because she has acquired a "private life," be it happy or sad, because this experience has "brought intelligence to a young girl. . . ." This notion of the acceptance of experience for its own sake, one of Colette's major themes in her nonfiction, is developed much more fully by the narrator "Colette" in *La Naissance du Jour.*

Gigi's education, presided over with great care and seriousness by her doting grandmother and her great-aunt, involves a series of concrete things that one must know, that one must do or not do. Gigi's scepticism in regard to this education is evident from the sarcastic tone in which she enumerates to Gaston some of the "Do's" and "Don't's." Above all, the principle is impressed on Gigi that the women in her family do not marry.

Gigi, the victim of a plot, triumphs over the conspirators. This plot, first conceived by Aunt Alicia when Gigi arrives at her apartment in Gaston's car, later carefully thought out by Alicia and Madame Alvarez and finally Gaston himself, is predestined to fail. Madame Alvarez has already failed with Gigi's mother, Andrée, who finds it less tiring to sing than to sleep for a living. What, of course, no one really took into account during the transaction was that Gaston loved Gigi and Gigi loved Gaston. The double surprise ending is the proof of this love and of the inadequacy of any rigorous principle in the guidance of someone else's life.

It would indeed be rare today to find someone who would cry, as did Marcel Proust,[3] while reading Mitsou's final letters to her lieutenant. The modern reader, on the other hand, would heartily agree with Proust in his criticism of the too pretty, too contrived, too affected passages which are found in Mitsou's often impossibly honest letters, and in his praise of the incomparable restaurant scene between Mitsou and her about-to-be lover. The lieutenant, like Gaston in *Gigi*, is an amusing, slightly ridiculous character, and it is in great part due to the way in which Colette portrays him that the novel escapes being oversentimental. His increasing uneasiness, as Mitsou candidly horrifies the waiter and the wine steward by her lack of sophistication and taste, becomes physical, to the extent indeed that the lieutenant begins to doubt whether he will be able to execute the ritual duties of a lover. This unexpected concern on the part of a bourgeois, rather stilted young man is an amusing and, at the same time, acute commentary on the elusive whys and wherefores of desire. Presented in some of their

more comic aspects, these whys and wherefores relieve
the heaviness that often accompanies the exaggeratedly
serious statements of the not too bright, but sincere
Mitsou.

Gigi is certainly the most humorous of Colette's fictional writings. All the characters in the novel participate in a bubbling comedy of manners. *Gigi* contains
none of the contrived sentences, the sentimental outbursts, that occur in *Mitsou*. Since Colette did not have
to worry about inventing a story, she was able to concen-
trate most of her attention on her characters. The result,
within a deliberately limited medium, is close to perfection.

Although Madame Alvarez and Alicia are very definitely ladies of the demimonde, they take from "Colette-
Sido" their enthusiasm and their attachment to the real.
Madame Alvarez, who "retained from her past life the
honorable habits of women who have lost their honor," [4]
is almost as wise in her domain as Sido in hers. If she
miscalculates in her judgment of Gigi, there is no malice
in her plotting, and the lessons and advice she gives Gigi
could be useful in almost any situation. Alicia, undoubtedly a more successful courtesan than her younger sister, to judge by the opulence of her apartment and the
variety of her jewels, is also more calculating, more
sophisticated and perhaps a bit less genuine. But she,
too, has been modeled after "Colette-Sido," and the two
sisters, together, are a formidable team. While they are
amusing because of the intensity which they display in
their pedagogic roles, their double link to the demimonde and to "Colette-Sido" gives them a naturalness
and a solidity which neither Mitsou nor even Gigi quite

achieves. The affection bestowed on them by their creator is second only to the affection bestowed on "Sido." This affection is, in Colette's world, a baptism which leads if not to immortality, almost inevitably to success.

When the "blue" lieutenant discovers Mitsou's crime is that "She makes you have to think about her just when you are tempted to say, 'You are only a little anxiety, you aren't big enough to be a real torment,' " [5] he has discovered a truth that applies, not only to Mitsou, but to all the "Colette-Claudines" and, by extension, to all the novels in which they appear. One is seduced without really wanting to be, without ever being quite sure of one's feelings, and, trying to escape, again seduced by an unexpected charm in author, in character or in style. But one is always aware of the fact that it is a seduction and not a deep love.

 **X**

Fanny, Jane, Alice and Julie

Everything that we love despoils us.[1]

The main characters in *La Seconde*, *Duo*, *Le Toutounier* and *Julie de Carneilhan* are women in their thirties or early forties (both they and Colette are very conscious of age), women who represent an intermediate stage between Colette's adolescents and her older women, but who, nonetheless, belong to the family "Colette-Sido." Fanny, Jane, Alice and Julie possess an unorthodox moral sense and tenacious endurance. They are highly capable females, endowed with hearty appetites and dependable digestions. They share with "Colette" the always amusing contrast between their earthy vitality and their complicated sentimental lives. Alice and Julie slap their thighs and then proceed to analyze, in the most lucid manner, the subtle changes in their feelings. They appraise the qualities of the body of a man who means nothing to them and shortly after declare in passionate outbursts that they are monogamous,

that they have loved and can love only one man. Alice's
tenderness for a wasp stuck in the marmalade, her myopic eyes, Julie's horror of a sickroom, her pleasure at
the evocation of childhood memories, her visits to the
fortuneteller, Fanny's inability "to be angry with Jane
who has such beautiful hair," to "scold Jean when he
has very blue eyes," [2] her attempts at concealing her
jealousy, are all almost direct references to incidents and
characteristics which Colette describes and notes in her
nonfiction as pertaining to her own life.

The important men in these novels, the popular playwright, Farou, in *La Seconde*, the director of theaters,
Michel, in *Duo*, and the right-wing deputy, Herbert
d'Espivant, in *Julie de Carneilhan*, bear a resemblance
to Colette's first husband, Monsieur Willy, to her second
husband, Henry de Jouvenel, and perhaps, in a lesser
degree, to her father, Jules Colette. Despite the differences in the actions in which they are involved, they are
all men of irresistible charm who lack moral courage,
that very courage which Colette has so generously bestowed on her female characters. The words "cheese it,
the cops," which both Farou and Michel unfailingly
repeat at certain given intervals, establish the existence
in these characters of a similar cast of mind. Not ad-
mitted into the company of the lucid and the strong, an
almost exclusively feminine company in Colette's world,
they bear the unattractive stigmata of vulgarity and
weakness. Much more than the women, these men remain prisoners of their exigent sensuality and their unlimited vanity. The total inferiority of Colette's men to
Colette's women is nowhere more evident than in the
portrayals of Michel and Herbert.

Suffering acutely from jealousy, Michel, unlike Fanny in *La Seconde*, cannot react against the poison. This condition is irremediable, because there is nothing within Michel, in his response either to life or to love, that can counteract the illness. In Colette's eyes, Michel's suicide is very clearly the result of a moral flaw. In general, Colette's men are more prone to contemplating or attempting suicide than are her women.

Herbert d'Espivant is the victor in his wily financial dealings with Julie de Carneilhan, but his victory is a sign of weakness and Julie's defeat a sign of strength. Herbert has used his charm and his cunning to deceive both Julie and his wife, deception being the only art in which he is proficient, whereas Julie, who was also guilty of blackmail, is exonerated by Colette because she was an accomplice through love.

Only Julie's brother, Léon de Carneilhan,[3] is immune from the vulgarity and weakness which plague the other members of his sex in these four novels. Léon's immunity derives, amusing though it may seem, from his all-consuming passion for his mares. Women play an insignificant role in his life, and this, it would seem, is the reason for Léon's strength. Colette appears to be saying that women in love surpass their natural mediocrity, whereas men lose whatever moral superiority they may have had. Women thrive in love, men wither.

The moral withering of the men does not in any way destroy their charm. Indeed, it may often enhance it by adding the piquant aroma of corruption. The "lesson" of *La Seconde* is that two women are often needed to control and to love one man, to counteract the terrible solitude of the couple from which, according to

Colette, women invariably suffer. This need for solidarity between women against men is also pointed out in *Duo*, when Maria, Michel's faithful housekeeper, turns against him and toward Alice when it becomes evident that both Michel's jealous suffering and his suicide are means by which he torments his wife. Such solidarity is one way for women to achieve an equilibrium in their love life, an equilibrium which all Colette's female characters, rarely her male characters, somehow achieve.

The milieus described in *La Seconde*, *Duo*, *Le Toutounier* and *Julie de Carneilhan* are, in appearance, though not in essence, different from those described in almost all of Colette's other novels. The term "bourgeois Bohemia" which Colette uses in *La Seconde* is also applicable to *Duo* and *Le Toutounier*. Fanny, Jane and Alice come from an impoverished bourgeois background, and their love affairs or marriages with theatrical men inevitably bring them and their bourgeois values into a bohemian environment. Julie de Carneilhan is the only one of Colette's major female characters who belongs to the French aristocracy. In Julie's case the aristocracy is very old, but because it is also very poor Julie associates with a strangely assorted group of people to whom the "bourgeois Bohemia" label may again be affixed.

These novels are not explicitly set in any one period, but with the aid of references to dress styles and prominent theatrical figures, it is possible to establish, without too much difficulty, the approximate historical time at which the action of the novels takes place: *La Seconde* in the late 1920's, *Duo* and *Le Toutounier* in the early 1930's, *Julie de Carneilhan* in the years preceding the second World War. The historical setting, though not the social setting, is less important in these novels than it is in *Mitsou* or *Gigi*. Fanny, Jane, Alice and Julie are not women of any particular era, although like all Colette's characters, they manifest very definite affinities with the milieu in which Colette and Monsieur Willy circulated. This is particularly evident in the often pointless references to Lesbianism which date these novels in a rather unfortunate way.

As the novels are all concerned with the outcome of a single, isolated situation, each is compressed into a short span of time—one summer in *La Seconde*, nine days in *Duo*, two days in *Le Toutounier* and about two weeks in *Julie de Carneilhan*. Colette tends to follow her characters very closely, from the time they rise in the morning until they go to bed at night. With the exception of an occasional restaurant scene, the action takes place entirely in a country house or a Paris apartment. No matter how severe the emotional strain under which the characters live, the reader is spared none of the details that compose the necessary routine of living: sleeping, washing, dressing, eating, cleaning, sewing. These details tend to give to Colette's novels a universality which neither the setting nor the action in which the characters are involved furnishes, and at the same time they serve as significant and intimate commentaries on a given character. The result is that whereas one could not imagine what a particular character would say on a topic of general interest, it is perfectly possible to describe how the character would act in a given situation and how he would look. The reader's knowledge of Colette's characters is always psychological and physical, never intellectual.

In each of these four novels the essential problem is the same: how to achieve equilibrium in an unbalanced situation, how to go on living when the ordered image of self and of the world which a human being carries is suddenly shattered.

Fanny Farou, one of the two heroines of *La Seconde*, is a dark, voluptuous woman of thirty-seven, who has been married for twelve years to a man known both for his talents as a playwright and the number of his mistresses. Farou's infidelities, frequent, shortlived and usually with young actresses, have become a ritual part of his family's life. Fanny accepts them out of habit and necessity.

When the novel begins, Fanny and her entourage, her sixteen-year-old stepson, Jean, and her husband's secretary and everyone's devoted friend and helper, Jane, are awaiting in a summer villa in Franche Comté a letter from Farou, who is in Paris. The rather complicated relationships and crossrelationships between the four characters are immediately made clear: Fanny loves her husband and is extremely fond of Jane; Farou loves Fanny and is extremely fond of Jane; Jean is in love with Jane; and Jane is extremely fond of Fanny and is in love with Farou. The last relationship is apparent to the reader before it is apparent to Fanny. Her discovery of the liaison between Jane and Farou and her handling of this delicate situation constitute the core of the novel.

It is through her stepson's adolescent and ferocious love for Jane that Fanny is forced to hear and to see, in the tone of their voices and their familiar gestures, that her husband and Jane are lovers. Accustomed to her hus-

band's infidelities outside the home, Fanny is ill-pre-
pared for what she considers to be a double treason and
the possible break-up of her life. Rather quickly, Fanny
installs herself in the "lucid and breathable atmosphere
of unhappiness." [4] Her senses and her mind more keenly
alert than before the discovery, Fanny takes the necessary time to observe, to think, to decide. Her main concern is with the care she must take to appear untroubled.

The culminating point of Fanny's suffering, when she
accidentally sees Farou kissing Jane, coincides with the
hectic preparations for the opening of Farou's latest
play. Fanny has made up her mind to have it out with
Jane and, if necessary, with Farou, once the play is
launched. The equanimity she manages to maintain despite great tension is brilliantly analyzed by Colette.

> She could not forgive her sorrow for being tolerable, for
> taking a place, between despair and indifference, in a spir-
> itual region which allowed for distractions, pleasures, scru-
> ples and compensations. She was constantly being aston-
> ished by the fact that the treason had not changed in her
> eyes either Farou or Jane.[5]

Fanny is saved by her very real, unchanging affection
for Farou and for Jane and by her honesty in admitting
that, despite her sorrow, life goes on. Jealousy, like other
forms of mental suffering, is both intense and intermittent. Because of the moments when she forgets,
Fanny is aware that there is in her a force more power-
ful than her suffering, which is, very simply, the desire
for a calm and ordered life.

The most interesting character in the novel is not
Fanny but Jane, beautiful, blond Jane, who came to replace a pregnant secretary and stayed forever. Practi-

cally and emotionally, Jane is an indispensable part
of the Farou household. To the average Anglo-Saxon
reader, her physical attentions to Fanny—touching
Fanny's hair, kissing Fanny's cheek, holding Fanny's
hand—might seem odd and excessive. But it must not
be forgotten that in Colette's world, feminine beauty
often evokes the same language and the same superficial
caresses in both men and women. Within Colette's fictional universe, there is not necessarily anything bizarre
in the tenderness and the compliments given to one
beautiful woman by another.

Jane is only too willing to continue in her role as
Fanny's intimate friend and Farou's occasional mistress.
And Fanny, at the end of the novel, implicitly proposes
this as the only possible solution. She tacitly accepts
Jane as her "second" in the love duel which she wages
with Farou; she tacitly accepts Jane as her companion
in solitude. This highly unconventional acquiescence to
a *ménage à trois* is made to appear quite normal and
rational within the given situation. A complex situation
cannot have a simple solution. Fanny prefers to save
what she can rather than to lose everything; she prefers
to attempt to live with the presence of the "other" rather
than to live alone.

Duo, Colette's most uncluttered novel, is an example
of what may happen to a person who does not have
Fanny's qualities. As the title indicates, there are two
major characters in the novel and their duet, from the
stylistic point of view, is harmonious. In terms of the
story the duet is discordant; and it ends with the abrupt
silence of one voice.

Duo is an almost clinical study of the cerebral and physical ravages of jealousy. Michel and Alice, happily married for ten years, are spending their Easter vacation at Michel's country home. The opening pages of the novel introduce the characters while they are still in a normal condition. It is completely by chance, in the middle of a conversation about producing a play for which Alice would design the costumes, that Michel insists on finding the purple blotter which Alice pretends has been misplaced. Michel's irate insistence is due in part to his fatigue (he has spent the morning wandering over his property with the caretaker), and in part to Alice's strange reactions, her curt dismissal of the blotter as an insignificant object while her dancing eyebrow and the "odor" of her fear betray her intense emotion. The blotter is discovered and in it a love letter written to Alice by one of Michel's associates. From the moment of discovery until the end of the novel, the reader witnesses the progress of Michel's illness, his mental and physical decline, the disintegration of a human being. Colette has managed to portray, not only Michel's plunge into obsession, but also Alice's reactions to his violent jealousy.

The united couple is slowly but surely sundered. Alice's immediate response is to reassure her husband that the short liaison, begun when she was ill and Michel was traveling, is already over, that it was never very important, that it merely arose from the need, while she was ill, for a tender confidant. Alice knows that Michel is suffering, and she attempts to alleviate this suffering both for his sake and for hers, for the salvation of their marriage.

But every word that Alice speaks, every gesture that

she makes is noted by Michel and interpreted in the light of his discovery. As he comes more and more to view Alice as a perennial source of torture, Alice becomes more and more impatient with his total unwillingness to cooperate in her efforts to "pick up the pieces," [6] more and more indifferent to what she considers to be her husband's self-inflicted pangs. His jealousy not only destroys Michel, it destroys everything around him. As if Michel had a repugnant contagious disease, the stench of his illness turns everyone away from him.

Michel and Alice's duet becomes increasingly dissonant, with the same jarring notes repeated at frequent intervals. From outside, the continual song of the nightingale, a song which accompanied their love-making the night before the discovery, now seems a cruel and insidious mockery of their love.

Michel succeeds in convincing both himself and Alice that if Alice had not been drawn to her lover through a tender friendship, but rather through an imperious physical need, he would understand, he would recover. Alice waits for what she hopes will be a propitious moment for her final confession of truth and the mitigation of Michel's pain. To prove to him that the liaison was indeed purely physical, Alice produces three letters written by her lover, three letters which the reader does not see but somehow follows as Michel avidly devours and then destroys them. Michel continues, however, to reread them in his mind and to visualize the detailed, explicit images that they contained. What he thought would be an antidote proves an even stronger poison. He drowns himself early the following morning.

The irony of this domestic tragedy has its origin in the always elusive matter of timing. After Michel has read the letters and felt their oppressive weight, he has a last moment of lucidity in which he realizes that, had he entered the room on that fatal day one half hour later, he might never have known of Alice's infidelity. Michel's timing, merely by chance, was bad; it cost him his life.

Le Toutounier is a sequel to *Duo*. The *"toutounier"* itself was alluded to in *Duo*, although the allusion becomes significant only when one has read both novels. Under the growing strain of her difficult marital situation, Alice wrote a letter to her three sisters in their Parisian *"toutounier." "Toutounier,"* a word invented by Colette, is the name which Alice and her sisters gave, as children, to the immense, old, leather sofa in their apartment. By extension, it has come to mean the home which they share and is the symbol of Alice's life before her marriage, of the "narrow fellowship," the "immodest and pure camaraderie" and the "mental and physical resemblance" [7] which united her and her three sisters. It is to the *"toutounier"* that Alice returns a few weeks after Michel's death.

There is no main action in *Le Toutounier*. The novel is composed of a series of incidents—the sisters eating, sleeping, dressing and chatting and an attempted assassination—which take place over a period of two days and which reveal the contrast between the world of the couple and the world of the family.

With her sisters, Alice quickly recaptures the *"toutounier* tone as they called an old liberty of joking without laughing, of not avoiding any subject of con-

versation, of keeping their composure in almost all circumstances, and of abstaining from tears." [8] The run-
down Paris apartment is Alice's refuge from the present,
the means by which she is able to find an equilibrium
through a return to her past.

Alice's sisters are "poor with elegance" and "courageous." The two who live at home work for their living
and are involved with married men. "We never resist a
man," says Alice. "We follow him everywhere except in
death." [9] In her relation to her dead husband, Alice vacil-
lates between an "unequal, capricious, badly subdued
sorrow" [10] and the notion that Michel's suicide was an
act of infidelity far graver than her own, a notion Colette obviously shares.

In *Le Toutounier*, the reader has the uncomfortable
feeling, despite reiteration by Alice and her sisters of the
importance in their lives of men and of having a man,
that they are much more at ease, much happier, in their
gynaeceum than outside it. Although they range in age
from twenty-nine to thirty-seven, they seem to be no
older than boarding-school girls. The novel suffers from
the somewhat precious and sentimental tone of their
dialogue, from their everlasting comments and observations on each others' eyes, hips, breasts and smells. This
overcharged feminine atmosphere which they have
maintained since childhood, since the period before men
assumed any importance for them, is one in which Alice
and her sisters flourish.

Le Toutounier ends with the projected departure of
Alice's two younger sisters, a third having already left,
and with Alice's decision to keep the *"toutounier"* going
in case they return. And there is no doubt that they will,

like Alice, eventually return. Where else and with whom else can they find the felicitous blend of comprehension and peace which characterizes their relationship to each other and to the *"toutounier"*? Certainly, in Colette's world, not with men.

Carneilhan, the dilapidated castle of Julie's family, is the *"toutounier"* of *Julie de Carneilhan*. It appears in the novel through evocation and description by Julie and her brother, Léon, and it is important as a symbol of strong, unbroken ties with the family and with the past. Like the *"toutounier,"* *Carneilhan* seems never to have known the presence of a mother-figure. Julie speaks of her father, who is still alive, and Alice speaks of her dead father, but neither of them ever mentions a mother. It is as if the maternal qualities had become associated with the home itself, had become, in short, home, with all that it implies of warmth and security. There is, moreover, a violent contrast between the world of *Carneilhan* and Julie's life in Paris, as there was between the atmosphere of *Le Toutounier* and that of *Duo*.

In the first two pages of the novel, Colette presents an amazingly complete portrait of her major character. The way in which Julie moves through the kitchen, sews, looks at herself in the mirror, dresses to go out and then sits straight in a chair, waiting for her friends, reveals the physical and moral qualities of a poor, aristocratic, beautiful, lonely, proud woman. This short, though careful, examination of the humdrum routine of Julie's existence is interrupted by the unexpected arrival of her brother. Léon brings news that will transform Julie's life.

Julie is the central figure of the novel, and through the people with whom she is involved the novel expands to include different milieus and different love intrigues. Léon brings in Julie's family background, *Carneilhan*, horses and the country. Her second husband, Herbert d'Espivant, from whom she has been divorced for three years, belongs to a wealthy, corrupt and aristocratic set. With Herbert's stepson, Toni, never directly presented in the novel, the reader enters into the strangely complex world of adolescent love. And through Coco Vatard, Julie's twenty-eight-year-old lover, and Lucie Albert, her cinema companion, there emerges the boring, workaday world of the petite bourgeoisie.

Despite this rather wide variety of incident and character *Julie de Carneilhan* is a very simply and skilfully composed novel. The first rapid presentation of Julie is followed by her cautious reaction to the news that her second husband is critically ill and to Léon's provocative suggestion that if Herbert dies, he might leave money to Julie. There is nothing either in Julie's words or in her gestures to indicate that anything other than Herbert's money could possibly arouse her.

The discovery made both by Julie and the reader, when Julie accepts Herbert's imperative call to lunch, is that Herbert, despite his illness, his cunning and his meanness, has not lost his power to seduce, his power to awaken, in Julie's apparently hardened heart, a cry of love. That Herbert is fully aware of his power, that he counted on Julie's love for the execution of a carefully contrived plan, is evident the moment he reveals his blackmail scheme to Julie at a second meeting. Julie, in a spontaneous act of love, consents to aid and abet the petty criminal.

Charmed by the luxuries of Herbert's home, full of pleasure and pride in thinking herself still loved and perhaps desired, Julie returns with distaste to her small studio apartment and to the irritating company of her young lover. She is sustained by expectancy; she is waiting for another sign from Herbert. The sign is not long in coming, but it is Marianne, Herbert's wife, not Herbert, who arrives at Julie's apartment. Faced with the exotic beauty of this wealthy, voluptuous woman and with the fact of Herbert's betrayal, Julie de Carneilhan momentarily loses her self-possession. But neither the deception nor her anger can bring her, in turn, to betray Herbert.

"O Herbert, my greatest love of all, happiest part of my life and my greatest sorrow," [11] cries Julie after Marianne's departure—as Renée once cried, as Colette may have cried. Julie's love for Herbert is still intact; he was "the man of her life," [12] the only real love, after which all others are meaningless. This is the cruel lesson which Julie learns. Her return to Carneilhan with Léon and his mares is the sign both of an abdication and an acceptance. Julie can no longer dally with the Coco Vatards; she can no longer bear the "moral solitude" of her city apartment. There can be no more love between Julie and a man, but there can be peace. To find peace, Julie goes home. Julie's final act brings us back to *La Retraite sentimentale* and closes one of Colette's fictional cycles.

 XI

Parables of Experience[1]

These pleasures which we lightly call physical. . . .[2]

Chéri, La fin de Chéri and *Le Blé en herbe* are more complex than the novels discussed so far and more profound than Colette's evaluation of them, in various interviews and in *Mes Cahiers*, might lead one to believe. If, in these three novels, Colette surpassed her intentions, it is because she was able to realize them without having recourse to banal psychological analysis and because she was able to preserve so skilfully both the particularities of her characters and their milieu and the more general significance of the dramas in which they are involved. The parable is always a symbolic story, and the danger for the writer is that the characters can easily become puppets manipulated with a specific end in view. Colette was naturally immune to this danger, because of her innate suspicion of abstraction and her strict adherence to the concrete. Chéri is a gigolo in love with an older woman, Philippe, in *Le Blé en herbe*, is an adolescent Parisian bourgeois in love with his childhood playmate, and neither of these characters ever loses the well-defined attributes of his background or the specific difficulties of his personal situation. At the same time, through Colette's art, they become representatives of an eternal drama, whose significance extends far beyond their own limited condition.

> *"Chéri and Léa are two orphans who meet."* [3]

Even though *Chéri* and *La fin de Chéri* were published six years apart, the two novels form one continuous love story. In *Chéri*, the twelve divisions, except for the next to the last, are short and could be taken by themselves as short stories. This may be explained very easily by the fact that *Chéri* first appeared in serial form in the magazine *La Vie Parisienne*. In *La fin de Chéri*, which was published only as a complete novel, most of the seven chapters are long.

The two novels tell the story of a love affair between a young gigolo, Chéri, and a middle-aged courtesan, Léa. The scene is Paris, the setting, the demimonde, the period, 1906–1919.

Time has been favorable to *Chéri* and *La fin de Chéri*. Published respectively in 1920 and 1926, they express for the contemporary reader a theme that was to dominate French literature in the 1930's and 1940's, the theme of the absurdity of man's life. Colette certainly never thought of her character, Chéri, as a vehicle for such a theme. If it is now possible to see in Chéri another image of the absurd hero or rather anti-hero, it is in part because the modern reader is accustomed to seeing absurd heroes, and in part because Chéri, prey both to boredom and to love, seems to be a victim of man's absurd condition. In reality, he is a victim only of his own absurd condition. Colette's humanity and Colette's skill are responsible for the illusion.

The character, Chéri, had haunted Colette since 1913, and he made his first appearance, under the name of Clouk, in a group of stories that she wrote for the newspaper *Le Matin*.[4] Clouk was a rich, ugly young man, suffering from bad adenoids; the name Clouk was derived from the sound made by his sniveling nose. With his mistress, Lulu, Clouk frequented the bars and nightclubs of pre-World War I Paris. But Colette soon tired of Clouk's ugliness, and he was re-created a thing of beauty, under the name of Chéri. Despite the fact that these first sketches, both of Clouk and of Chéri, are less bitter, less interesting, than the two novels which grew out of them, they already contain the central theme of the later novels: the "pure" and incurable love of a young man for an older woman.

Chéri seemed a very familiar figure to a certain reading public of the 1920's. The group of free-floating and troubled young people of postwar Paris, who moved from bar to bar, saturated with drink and hypnotized by the newly imported jazz, found in Chéri's life an image of their own lives, centered on love affairs and alcohol and vividly described in the novels of such writers as Drieu La Rochelle and Paul Morand. Chéri's contemporaries, like today's generation, were reading meanings into and not out of the novel. They were fooled by the fact that Chéri, too, had a mistress, that Chéri, too, had a lovely wife whom he left, that Chéri, too, fought in the war, that Chéri, too, drank in bars. They were fooled by Colette's careful documentation of her novel within a definite historical period, fooled by surface realities. Chéri is at the same time a most ordinary and a most unusual case. He is nothing more than a very handsome, very spoiled, almost completely inarticulate young man, who falls in love once and forever. The relation between Chéri's mediocrity and Chéri's passion is of the utmost importance.

It would be difficult to summarize Chéri's situation more succinctly than Colette has done:

> I simply wanted to say that when a middle-aged woman has a liaison with a very young man, she runs less of a risk than he of remaining ineffaceably marked by it. No matter what he does, through all the liaisons that will follow, he will be unable not to evoke the memory of his old mistress.[5]

A very specific factor, the difference in age between the middle-aged mistress, Léa, and the very young man, Chéri, is thus the principal source of the drama. In Léa's and Chéri's reactions to their unavoidable separation lie the action and the moral. The novels deal with the successive breakdowns, first of Léa and then of Chéri, after the latter's marriage to Edmée, the daughter of still another aging courtesan. Léa survives; Chéri kills himself.

In the first pages of *Chéri*, Colette introduces the major characters, themes and incidents of the novels in terms of one object: Léa's pearl necklace.

"Léa! Give it to me, your pearl necklace! Do you hear me, Léa? Give me your necklace!"

No answer came from the large, wrought-iron and brass-sculpted bed which shone in the shadow like a coat of armor.[6]

The pearl necklace and the bed set the stage, not only for the opening scene, but for the entire action. From the large bed which is Léa's coat of armor, the arena of her love battle, comes a "feminine voice," and there appear two "magnificent" naked arms, "two beautiful but lazy hands." In front of a large mirror dances a "gracious devil," wearing silk pyjamas and a pearl necklace. The vain, preening male, displaying charms whose power is obviously unquestioned, is Chéri.

That this "very handsome and very young man" should be wearing and wanting to keep a pearl necklace, is already an indication of Chéri's particular character. The pearls please him because he knows their value, because he finds them becoming and because he would like them for his wedding trousseau. They are all the more important to him because they were given to Léa by a former lover. Thus, in a very few lines and indirectly, the milieu is established.

But the pearls reveal still more. Léa no longer wears them to bed at night because, should Chéri wish to play with them in the early morning, he would see her aging neck. Chéri's approaching marriage, Léa's age, Chéri's latent jealousy, Léa's indulgence, their mutual understanding, indeed the very stuff of which the novel is composed, may be deduced from the incident of the pearl necklace.

The necklace reappears throughout *Chéri* and *La fin*

de Chéri as an instrument of spiritual torture. Every pearl necklace that Chéri sees reminds him of Léa, of the absence of Léa in his life.

Chéri is one of the few novels in which Colette uses the flash-back technique. After three scenes which show the characters in their present situation, she quickly sketches in the essential features of Léa's past, Chéri's past and the beginning of their liaison.

Léonie Wallon, called Léa de Lonval, has always been a successful courtesan, an artiste in her chosen field. "She liked order, beautiful linen, old wines, a careful cuisine." [7] Although Léa has never given herself to a man she did not love, she has managed to avoid great sorrows. Her unfailing sense of propriety and measure, of what is done and what is not done, has saved her beauty, her money and her independence from the fate that awaits most Léas at the approach of middle age.

Colette has endowed Léa with all the external qualities necessary for a courtesan: beauty, expensive clothes and jewels, a private *hôtel* in Paris, an impressive list of lovers. She has also endowed Léa with an abundance of common sense. Léa is a veritable mine of advice on very practical matters: constipation, perspiration, color combinations, food combinations. Her comments to Chéri on the spiritual sickness of the young in postwar Paris is something of a philosophical testament: "Romanticism, neuroses, the disgust of life: stomach." [8] Léa is one of the most solid members of the "Colette-Sido" clan.

Fred Peloux, later known as Chéri, is the son of one of Léa's acquaintances. Brought up by chambermaids and valets, alternately forgotten and then spoiled and pampered, Chéri is treated by his entourage much as one might treat an exquisite animal. Colette's constant recourse to the animal world when she wishes to find appropriate images for describing Chéri's face, Chéri's gestures or Chéri's poses accentuates the fact that Chéri is perhaps something more, perhaps something less, than human. Accustomed to wealth, accustomed to satisfying all the superfluous needs of his very demanding and totally undisciplined nature, Chéri is, at least in appearance, the flower of all gigolos, the ideal lover for a courtesan.

Léa and Chéri fell into each other's arms, out of boredom, in 1906. Léa was then forty-three and Chéri, nineteen. One night, when Léa was paying a ritual visit to her old friendly enemy, Charlotte Peloux, Chéri's mother unexpectedly left the room. Chéri demanded a kiss, Léa liked his mouth, Chéri demanded another, and Léa, determined to use all her art, kissed him too well. Their liaison, which was to last six years, had started. The "end" of Chéri is already foreseen at the end of the second kiss.

> . . . he held out his arms to her, opened his beautiful, uncertain hands, threw back a wounded head and showed, between his eyelashes, the double sparkle of two tears, while he murmured words, laments, an animal and amorous chant, in which she distinguished her name, *"chérie,"* "come," "never leave you again," a chant to which she listened, leaning over him and full of anxiety, as if she had, inadvertently, hurt him badly.[9]

It is not by his sexual prowess that Chéri becomes so precious to Léa, but rather by his impetuosity, his tenderness and his need for her. Chéri is, for Léa, child, pupil and lover; Léa is, for Chéri, mother, teacher and lover. Psychologically, socially and physically, the balance is perfect.

During the six years which they spend together, Léa and Chéri create around themselves a sensual paradise whose setting is an elaborate bedroom in which the main prop is Léa's immense bed. They eat and drink like gourmets. They pass endless time on the care of their bodies and the calculating of household expenses. Money, jewels, clothes, foods, the liaisons of their acquaintances are the topics about which they, like the other members of their world, converse.

Within their own marginal social group, Chéri and Léa are, aside from their outstanding beauty, very ordinary people. For the average reader, too, they seem in their conversations and preoccupations ordinary almost to the point of vulgarity. But by the quality and quantity of their passion, Chéri and Léa transcend the limits of their milieu and its conventions. In this closed, restricted world, apparently impervious to anything but the sensual, the very real tie that binds Chéri to Léa and Léa to Chéri is slowly formed. This tie is somehow of a different order from that created by the repeated patterns and habits of their everyday life. The nature and strength of this tie are progressively revealed in *Chéri*. In *La fin de Chéri*, its tragic effect becomes apparent.

Colette's method, in *Chéri*, is a simple one. The major characters are seen first together in their daily lives, then separately, as each attempts to live without the other, then again together. And it is during the period of separation that each becomes more lucid, more articulate. Brought face to face in the last scenes of the novel, they confront each other with a new perception and a new awareness.

Colette manages to maintain an often difficult equilibrium between the serious and comic aspects of her two novels. Although Colette's is very far from the romanticized version of the demimonde as presented by certain nineteenth-century writers, she is obviously very familiar with and very fond of her characters.

In the *Claudine* novels, the characters were targets for Colette's quips and Colette's disdain. Their vices were treated as ludicrous and they themselves as nothing more than vehicles for these vices. In *Chéri* and *La fin de Chéri*, it is the total character, not merely his or her vice, that is humorous. Colette no longer desires to shock the reader or to poke fun at her creations. One has the feeling that in the setting described, gigolos, Lesbians and opium smokers are as normal as would be, in another setting, bored married couples and martini drinkers.

Most of the secondary characters in *Chéri* and *La fin de Chéri* are female and well past middle age. Seen together, they seem very much like any other elderly ladies who spend their time playing cards and chatting —with the difference, of course, that Colette's ladies are infinitely more amusing and more human.

The humor derived from Léa's reflections on her advancing age, Chéri's lyrical descriptions of his own beauty, Charlotte Peloux's biting and witty remarks to her friends, La Baronne de la Berche's virile comments on women, Lili's love talk with her young lover, is never malicious. At certain moments, each of these characters is somewhat grotesque, something of a caricature. But since they are all able to accept as well as to return insults, since they spare neither themselves nor others, laughter at them is never mockery.

Colette's humor is partially responsible for her characters' credibility. Could one not, on occasion, laugh at Chéri, he would be a most unbearable young man. If he succeeds in endearing himself to the reader, it is precisely because he is often ridiculous. In Chéri's case, the ridiculous and the pathetic are closely allied. Their source lies in the image Chéri has of himself as Léa's beauteous child-lover and the failure of his attempts to impose this image on his young wife. When he tells Edmée that his face is handsome because his eyes have the shape of a sole and his mouth that of the number 3 lying on its side, Chéri unwittingly reduces himself to the absurd. Edmée's refusal to accept this image is shared by the reader, who sees Chéri for what he really is, a pathetically comical gigolo.

Most of the humor in the two novels comes from the strange mixture of nonconformity and conformity which characterizes the demimonde. The language of that world has a distinctive flavor, in which the utmost candor mingles with a certain reticence, a language through which the unexpected and often rigid morality of the "immoral" may be perceived.

> Her [Léa's] young lover had never come upon her when she was without make-up, or with her blouse unbuttoned, or in her bedroom slippers during the day. "Naked, if one wishes," she would say, "but not half-dressed." [10]

The combination of Léa's sane, healthy outlook and her status and role in society is responsible both for her success as a character and her survival as a woman. After

Chéri's marriage, Léa begins the long combat with her-self, a combat from which, thanks to her great experi-ence as a courtesan and her very solid hold on life, she slowly but surely emerges victorious.

The loss of Chéri is for Léa a terrible loss. Léa's suffer-ing is physical in nature, as Léa's joys are physical. But despite the fact that this suffering is acute, more acute than anything Léa has ever known, she refuses to submit to it. Recognizing her pain and its cause, Léa leaves Paris for a change of air.

Colette has very deftly plotted the relation between the main action, the love of Léa and Chéri, and the love involvements of the minor characters who appear in the novel. In the period that follows Chéri's marriage and before Léa decides to leave Paris, she spends an evening at the home of Madame Peloux. Léa is repulsed by the presence of Lili, aged seventy, and her adolescent lover, the Italian Prince Ceste. Lili and her lover are indeed pathetically grotesque, and to Léa they are a startling example of what she and Chéri might have become. The difference between Léa and Lili is that for Léa, love-making must cease when beauty fades. This is part of Léa's code, a code that not only saves her from ridicule, but adds to her personality a moral tone which is more elevated than that of her cronies. Léa knows that for all things there is a time and a place. It is not always suf-ficient to know. Léa, with difficulty, also accepts.

The difference in the way Léa and Chéri react to their suffering is vast, and in this difference lies the secret of Léa's survival and Chéri's death. Chéri returns from his honeymoon of two and a half months nervous and tired. He refuses to show any interest in his wife or in his new

home. Only the enigmatic note which Léa sent his
mother before she left Paris arouses Chéri's curiosity.
This curiosity, this unvoiced though evident preoccupation with Léa, is carried into and colors his relations
with his wife, Edmée. Lovely, young, sweet, but incapable of paying Chéri the detailed physical compliments he demands, loving and jealous, but unable to be
mother, teacher and lover, Edmée fails in every way to
give Chéri that all-important image of himself which he
derived from Léa's love.

Unable to discover Léa's whereabouts, Chéri leaves
home. With his friend, Desmond, he haunts the nightclubs and vice dens of Paris. One evening, Chéri sees
lights in Léa's *hôtel*. " 'Ah!,' he said softly, 'that is happiness?—I didn't know.' " [11] Laden down with gifts, he
returns to his wife. Chéri never attributes his changing
moods, his sudden depressions and exaltations, to any
one cause. Indeed, Chéri never thinks, never reasons. He
feels, or he vaguely imagines. Never, in any way, does
Chéri attempt to change his state. He merely gives in to
it and waits for outside circumstances to give him a new
direction. It takes Chéri a very long time to understand
the depth of his love for Léa.

Léa's awareness develops as her unbearable solitude
grows. After a rather dull trip, she has returned to Paris,
prepared to reduce her life to evening bridge parties
with her cronies. But never for a moment does she cease
to think of Chéri. "My poor Chéri, isn't it funny to think
that the two of us—you by losing your old mistress, and
I by losing my scandalous young lover—have each lost
the most honorable thing that we possessed on earth." [12]
Honorable, because in the game of love as it was played

by Léa and Chéri, there was a kind of purity that came
from a mutual tenderness, a mutual respect. Honorable,
because together, Léa and Chéri both observed the rules
of the game.

The final scenes of the novel are trial scenes both for
Léa and Chéri. In these scenes, all that has remained
unspoken is said, all that has been pain momentarily
disappears, to become pain again, lucidity temporarily
bows to illusion and illusion is extinguished, and all that
is most honorable in the character of Léa de Lonval is
revealed.

One evening at midnight, Léa's doorbell rings. Chéri
has returned. The opening small talk and banter, due
in part to habit and in part to their mutual uneasiness,
cease abruptly as Chéri throws himself sobbing and
stammering upon Léa. " 'I find you again! my Nounoune! O my Nounoune, your shoulder, and your same
perfume, and your necklace, my Nounoune, ah! it's terrific—and the little burnt taste in your hair, ah, it's—it's
terrific.' " [13]

This litany of the rediscovery of Léa through touch,
smell, sight and taste, punctuated by the very banal
"terrific," has a counterpart in Léa's words: " 'My little
one—my bad one—here you are—here you are back
again—what have you done? You are so bad—my beauty. . . . Wicked beast, little heartless devil.' " [14] In the
intimate tenderness of this moment, Léa asks Chéri:
" 'So you loved me?' He lowered his eyes with a childish
confusion: 'Yes Nounoune!' A little burst of strangled
laughter, that she could not hold back, warned Léa that
she was very close to giving in to the most terrible joy
of her life." [15] What Léa and Chéri find in each other is

a gift which they give one to the other, the gift of iden-
tification, of an image of self. Chéri gives to Léa her
femininity; Léa gives to Chéri his diabolical beauty. But
also, for the first time, they announce their love for each
other, Chéri, in answer to a question, and Léa, when she
admits that she has no new lover. Lying in bed after their
love-making, Léa abandons herself to the idea that Chéri
has come back forever.

With morning comes a new revelation. Chéri pretends
to be asleep, but he is spying on Léa, on Léa's age. She
is unpowdered, uncombed; her double chin and ringed
neck come between Chéri and his happy vision of the
previous evening. The more Léa speaks of their future
plans, of her love for him, the more Chéri withdraws
from Léa's world, the less he desires to be treated as an
incapable adolescent. As Léa senses Chéri's withdrawal,
she becomes violent, voluble and insulting. It is Chéri
who calls her back to her own code of honor. And then
all is said or implied: how Chéri missed Léa, how he
wanted her, how he thought of her, and how he found
her aged. Léa heroically takes upon herself the responsibility for their impossible situation: "I never spoke
to you about the future. Forgive me, Chéri; I loved
you as if we were both to die within the next hour. Because I was born twenty-four years before you, I was
condemned, and I dragged you down with me——" [16]
Léa foresees all Chéri's suffering. In her sorrow and her
grandeur, she has become a kind of prophetess, to whom
the meaning of things past and the weight of things to
come are suddenly made clear. To such heights has the
courtesan of the opening pages risen.

At the end of *Chéri*, it is Léa who suffers. She suffers,

not only because Chéri leaves her, but because his departure signalizes her death as a lover, as a woman. The tie that bound Léa to Chéri was not merely a physical tie, but rather a tie based on the complex notion of self and security. When Chéri goes, Léa's perfume goes, her femininity goes, because they no longer receive the objective confirmation necessary to their existence. Chéri's departure coincides with the end of Léa's sexual life.

Chéri's love for Léa has been temporarily muted by his disillusionment, his sudden awareness of Léa's age. But in *La fin de Chéri* he is suffering as Léa suffered at the end of *Chéri*, suffering because he cannot live without that image of himself and the world created around it which only Léa can give him.

The first World War separates *Chéri* and *La fin de Chéri*. In this second novel, inferior to the first as are all of Colette's sequels, the story of Chéri is played out against the background of postwar Paris, a Paris of hectic dancing and drinking, of speculation and easy money. As the novel opens, Chéri is, as he was at the end of the first volume, alone in the night air. If, at the end of the first novel, one might have thought that Chéri was moving toward a new life, this illusion is quickly dispelled. "Ah! It's nice out. . . . No, it is not," [17] says Chéri, breathing the evening air, and this indecision, this inability to come to terms with a simple state of feeling, characterizes his drifting, solitary condition. In the opening scene of *La fin de Chéri*, Chéri is presented as an "outsider," as a "stranger." He is standing near his opulent house on the avenue Henri-Martin, and as he answers Edmée's clear, questioning voice, which comes down to him from a second floor window, it is apparent that the strained relations between them have not changed, except that now Edmée seems in complete control of herself. Caught up in the war effort, in hospital work, she has become a busy woman of the world, busy, too, with a liaison. Madame Peloux is also very much engaged in doing "good," in receiving honorary ribbons, and in making money. The demimonde is dying out; it is becoming bourgeois. All this earnest female activity, all the changes in a way of life, brought about by the war, only help to increase Chéri's melancholy, to make him feel even more of an outsider.

What is really at the root of Chéri's *vague à l'âme* is revealed only gradually, or rather the external causes are revealed before the real one. And it is because of these external causes that certain critics have seen in Chéri a precursor of the existentialist hero. Chéri fought in the war and survived an explosion which killed his friend, Pierquin. The force of the explosion threw Pierquin's body on top of Chéri, protecting him like a shield. Chéri is in the position of a soldier who comes back from absurd and hideous scenes of death to an overly patriotic, socially active wife and mother, with whose hectic life he is unable to cope. His disgust at what he considers the phony activities of Edmée, Charlotte Peloux and their friends, his refusal to partake of their world, are all condensed in his answer to his mother, when she asks him the traditional "What's the matter?"

"The matter is that everyone is a no-good louse." [18]

But Chéri's real drama is not based on any sudden realization of the absurdity of human life and activity; his floundering state, his nausea, are not based on any metaphysical awareness. A female voice which, from the shadows on his evening walk, calls out to him, "Hi, kid," is an omen of things to come. Chéri trembles at the word "kid," because this word, like any word or object which has a profound effect on him, is associated with Léa. And indeed it is only when he can speak with his friend, Desmond, about Léa, or when, in old Camille de la Berche, he finds a reflection of his own solitude, that Chéri seems to emerge from his terrible apathy. His preoccupation with Léa grows as the novel progresses, and with Léa Chéri associates his lost childhood, his lost adolescence. Chéri's incapacity to live in the postwar Paris of 1919 is only superficially connected with his war experiences or his domestic difficulties. It is very simply that he is incapable of living outside that world which Léa created for him, a world in which he could be and indeed had to be the "bad kid," the beautiful devil, the impetuous and all-admired child. The complicating factor is that, unlike Léa, Chéri either cannot be or refuses to be clear-minded enough to understand the reason for this insurmountable wall which separates him from society.

As in *Cheri*, it is Charlotte Peloux who paves the way for the scene between Chéri and Léa. Upset by her son's obvious unhappiness, almost distracted when he reveals to her his total distaste for women, she phones Léa in Chéri's presence, thereby indicating to her son what she thinks is the road to salvation.

Chéri's meeting with Léa is, for him, fatal. Five years have elapsed since he voluntarily left the arms and the bed of a woman whose beauty was fading. He finds now an immense, gray-haired lady, recognizable only by her voice, the blue of her eyes and her pearl necklace. In the presence of this old, healthy and sexless woman who, while calmly discussing with a crony the qualities necessary to perfect male beauty, admits that she once loved Chéri, his agitation and despair mount. Unable to accept that this is really Léa, he tries to believe that it is a masquerade, that somehow, somewhere, beneath all the flesh and wrinkles, his Léa will reappear. But the enormous mass remains.

No real contact is possible between this elderly woman, who appears to have stoically accepted her fate, and this thirty-year-old "boy" who is desperately searching for his past. And so, for the last time, Chéri leaves Léa. This all-important scene is placed in almost the exact middle of the novel. What follows is the slow, poisonous effect the memory of the scene has on an already listless and morbid Chéri.

The monotony of his daily routine of doing nothing, his moral indignation at himself for compromising with a wife whom he does not love, his disgust with his mother for her financial deals and with the world in general for its lack of purity, his endless daydreaming about Léa, lead Chéri from despair to a kind of clarity. He sees the future as an endless repetition of the present, he sees the future forever void of Léa, and he regrets that when he went to see her five years ago, he did not stay. And as the beauty of his princely, voluptuous adolescence spent with Léa passes through his mind, he cries, " 'Everything's gone to hell. I'm thirty years old. For me,' finished Chéri, 'I'm pretty sure there's nothing else to say.' " [19]

Chéri's meeting with La Copine, another of his mother's contemporaries, provides him with a refuge for a time.

La Copine, now old and miserable, lives in the past, talks of the past, talks of Léa as Chéri knew her and of the younger Léa whom Chéri did not know. Through her endlessly repeated anecdotes, La Copine helps Chéri to keep alive by feeding his cult. Chéri's last month is spent in her oriental salon, listening to her stories and gazing at the pictures of Léa which adorn the walls. But La Copine is forced to go away for a few days, and when Chéri finds himself alone in her apartment, he realizes the end has come. La Copine, when she returns, can only continue to retell the same tales; and Chéri can never again have Léa. Chéri's lucidity before his final act, his awareness of all that Léa meant to him, is all the more violent because he came to it with such difficulty. "But because you were born so long before me, because I loved you above all other women, we have been well punished. Look at you, shamefully finished and consoled, and me——me, while others say: there was the war, I can say: there was Léa." [20] His last words are "Nounoune——my Nounoune," and his index finger presses on the trigger of a small, black revolver.

Inherent in Chéri's final act are the refusal and inability to compromise with reality so characteristic of the romantic hero. "I therefore got rid of Chéri," says Colette in an interview, "in order to assure him, at least in the other world, of the company of the pure. I beg you to forgive me, but I believe that Chéri's purity existed a little, if only in my imagination." [21]

It is rare that a novel by Colette should remind one of a work by another author, but there is a rather striking similarity between *Chéri* and *La fin de Chéri* and a short story, *La Femme abandonnée* (1832), written by

Colette's favorite novelist, Balzac. *La Femme aban-donnée*, according to Balzac, is the story of a spiritual crime. Gaston de Nueil promises eternal love and devotion to a once abandoned woman, Madame de Beauséant. After nine years of happiness, he leaves her to marry a young heiress whom he does not love. When, unable to live without his former mistress, he attempts to see her, she refuses. Gaston, because of his sorrow and also because, in leaving Madame de Beauséant, he committed a crime, kills himself. The difference in milieu and emphasis notwithstanding, the similarity between the outer pattern of events in the two works seems a little more than fortuitous. It is, however, unlikely that Colette conceived of Chéri's death as a punishment for having left Léa. Chéri's death, as Colette herself declares, is a consecration of his purity, and, it might be added, the apotheosis of his love. It is the only gesture that could have saved Chéri from his terrible mediocrity.

> *More than any other natural phenomenon, I have all my life passionately observed the moments of unfolding. It is in them that resides for me the essential drama, rather than in death which is only a banal defeat.*[22]

The original publication of *Le Blé en herbe* as a magazine serial explains the novel's composition. Since it was to appear in installments, each chapter had its own title and each chapter but the last was in itself a small but compact whole.[23] However, when it became clear to the publishers of the magazine that Colette intended to have her adolescent hero and heroine make love at the end of the novel, they decided against continuing publication. Since Colette was no longer under the obligation to cut to fit their space requirements, the last chapter is by far the longest in the book. The outside circumstances which conditioned the form the novel was to take are all the more significant since one might be tempted, if unaware of these circumstances, to praise the logic of what would appear to be Colette's planned compositional device: sixteen short chapters which set the stage and then the denouement. Chance has once again been favorable to Colette.

Le Blé en herbe is, like *Chéri* and *La fin de Chéri*, a love story. The entire action takes place in Brittany at the end of a summer's vacation. For fifteen years, the Ferret family and the Audibert family have together rented a villa by the sea, and for fifteen years, Vinca, now fifteen and a half, and Philippe, now sixteen and a half, have played together, have planned their future together. This particular summer, or rather end of summer, differs from the others in that both Philippe and Vinca have passed from childhood to adolescence. They are on the threshold of a new world, the world of physical love. "All their childhood united them, adolescence separates them." [24] Therein lies the drama. In the course of the novel, Philippe and Vinca do exactly the same things they have always done together during the summer: they swim; they fish; they sunbathe; they go on picnics. But their most ordinary gestures and words have become self-conscious, and the presence of Eros is always between them.

As Lycenion, in *Daphnis and Chloë*, initiates Daphnis

in love, so it is an older woman, a stranger, who introduces Philippe to the world of physical love and it is Philippe who, in turn, initiates Vinca. There are other similarities between *Le Blé en herbe* and Longus's novel, *Daphnis and Chloë*.[25] Both concern adolescent love, and the adolescents in these two novels are in direct contact with nature. But although it is evident that Colette knew of *Daphnis and Chloë*,[26] it is doubtful that she deliberately intended her own story to be a modern version of the Greek.

The novel's three principal characters, Philippe, Vinca and Madame Dalleray, live in a tightly closed world. Philippe and Vinca refer to the members of their respective families as "the shadows." The "shadowy" existence of this adult bourgeois world serves a double purpose in the novel. Philippe and Vinca, although they partake in certain family activities, are completely isolated by their own preoccupations from the banter of their elders. And yet Colette makes it abundantly clear that, children of this very bourgeois milieu, they are themselves extremely bourgeois. When Vinca thinks of the future or plans for it, she sees it in terms of a marriage with Philippe and a kind of routine or pattern of events which in no way differs from that of her family. Because of their age, because of their passion, Vinca and Philippe rise, like small deities, above their environment; they are in a temporary state of grace. Five or six years later, there would be no novel to write.

In *Le Blé en herbe*, Colette has used the same device as in *Chéri*. She has taken two characters who, within their own milieu, are ordinary, but she has set them apart, she has isolated them from their milieu, through the miracle of love. Into this closed, adolescent world, Colette introduces Madame Dalleray. Seen only once by Vinca, but immediately recognized as a potential enemy, Madame Dalleray has a threefold function in the novel. She initiates Philippe into the world of physical love; she awakens Vinca's violent jealousy; and she represents a form of love, or rather an attitude toward love, which enlarges the novel's central theme. Although Colette focuses the reader's attention on the "game of love" as it is played between Philippe and Vinca, she also provides glimpses of other forms of love: the almost inarticulate affection of Monsieur Audibert for his son; the clannish attachment of Vinca for her family; the seemingly generous and altruistic love of Madame Dalleray for Philippe. These other loves find their expression in broken phrases and in gestures, whereas the hero and heroine are, at times, gifted with the tongues of poets, or rather with the tongue of Colette. It is through this very mixture of everyday speech and poetic language that the novel gains its force and that Philippe and Vinca become symbolic characters. The poetry emerges in certain speeches made by Philippe and Vinca, speeches usually uttered in solitude, and through the constant commentaries of the omniscient author. As, step by step, Philippe and Vinca experience the immense range of feelings that a love relationship can arouse—desire, repulsion, suspicion, jealousy, satisfaction—Colette is there to point from the particular to the general, to make of Philippe a symbol of all men and of Vinca a symbol of all women.

On the second page of the novel, Philippe is introduced as "subtle, born for the hunt and for deceit." [27]

When Philippe impatiently and angrily tells Vinca how tired he is of waiting, of waiting to be more than half a man, Colette both comments on his attitude and poetizes it: "He radiated intolerance, and a kind of traditional despair. The haste to grow older, the scorn for a period in which body and soul flower, changed this child of a small Parisian manufacturer into a Romantic hero." [28] This poetization of the hero is carried on throughout the novel, as Colette changes the images used to describe Philippe. He is in turn: "less ignorant than Daphnis"; "an oriental prince"; "an orphan prince"; "a Latin God"; "an angry God"; "a very ancient and very wild Phil." Madame Dalleray and Vinca are also poetized, but to a lesser degree. For Philippe, Madame Dalleray is "The Lady in White," (she was dressed completely in white the first time he saw her); she is also "a beautiful, authoritative demon," "the mistress," or "the master." This last image corresponds to the author's view of Madame Dalleray, for Colette, in describing her, almost never fails to use the adjective "virile." "She joked in a virile manner"; she always has "a virile smile." This mingling of male and female elements is not limited to descriptions of Madame Dalleray. After his first night of love, Philippe, looking in the mirror for signs of his new masculinity, discovers that his face is like that of "an exhausted young girl." Philippe's adventure, while consecrating his masculinity, arouses a latent, strong feminine sensitivity.

Vinca is "The Periwinkle," "The Doe," "The Child." She, too, occasionally is assigned masculine attributes, but the images associated with Vinca are mostly those related to the feminine principle. At the beginning of

the novel, before Philippe's liaison with Madame Dalleray, Vinca wants to die, to commit suicide with Philippe, as a romantic apotheosis of their impossible passion. But when she discovers Philippe's infidelity, she
no longer wishes to die. Colette comments on Vinca's
attitude and Philippe's incapacity to understand it.
"Peevish, he misjudged the mission of enduring, vested
in all the female species, and the sacred instinct of in-
stalling oneself in unhappiness and exploiting it like a
mine of precious materials. The evening and fatigue
helping, he was worn out by this bellicose child who was
fighting in primitive style for the salvation of a couple." [29]

This poetic rendering of the adolescent love between
two bourgeois Parisians at the end of a summer's vacation is not without its irony. When Philippe and Vinca
decide to speak, Philippe about his liaison and Vinca
about her intuitions and her suffering, Colette prefaces
their dialogue with this comment: "They felt a bitter
and identical satisfaction in going, with the very first
words of their conversation, beyond the commonplaces
of dispute and of lies. It is peculiar to heroes, actors and
children, to feel at ease on an elevated plane. These children foolishly hoped that a noble sorrow might be born
from love." [30] In *Chéri* and *La fin de Chéri*, Colette's
real subject seemed to be the nature of love, the nature
of the tie that binds two people together. In *Le Blé en
herbe*, Colette's real subject would seem to be the meaning of love. And the meaning is essentially that love is
a game, a game played by predestined partners, whose
roles have long since been prepared for them. As Colette never tires of saying, love has only one kind of

language; the love experience is always the same experience. Hence, she is free to compare Philippe to a romantic hero, to a god, to Daphnis, and Vinca to all women. The irony lies in the fact that Philippe and Vinca think that they are unique, that they are for the first time inventing love and its joys and sufferings. Colette, with her accumulated images and comparisons, has taken great pains to show that the exact opposite is true, and that at every step of the way, at those very moments when Philippe and Vinca feel that they are discovering new worlds and reaching new heights, they are following an old pattern, they are moving on a much-travelled road.

Chéri, *La fin de Chéri*, *Le Blé en herbe*, three slim volumes, two short love stories and yet two parables on the nature and meaning of love. Love cannot last, for we seek in love an image of ourselves which the beloved, in time, can no longer give us. Love is a game, the most banal, the oldest of games, and yet it is only through this very ordinary experience that the characters transcend both their milieu and their own natures, that courtesan, gigolo and Parisian adolescents are momentarily transfigured, that they are at the same time themselves and idealizations of themselves. And as idealizations of themselves, they become prototypes, and as prototypes, they exemplify, they become the figures of the parable, figures from whose experience there emerges a truth.

It is important, however, not to claim for these novels a place that they do not deserve. Within the limits of the milieu chosen, the characters presented and the drama enacted, Colette is eminently successful. But the milieu and the characters contain their own limitations. *Chéri, La fin de Chéri* and *Le Blé en herbe* are the best of Colette's novels and they are very good novels, but they are not great. Beyond the question of the depth of the author's vision, a great novel demands, essentially, a character who can support the weight of the adjective. Only two of Colette's characters, the true "Colette-Claudine" and the true "Colette-Sido" can support this weight, but both significantly and unfortunately neither the true "Colette-Claudine" nor the true "Colette-Sido" are to be found in her novels.

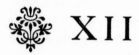 XII

Hide-and-Seek

"What did you say, my Dédé?"
"Oh! nothing. . . ." [1]

The *nouvelle*, or short story, was originally an anecdote
based on a real event, purportedly related by someone
who was present at the time the event took place. Today,
the short story is usually defined as a brief work of fiction, rigorously composed, concerned, as a rule, with a
single episode and sustained by a unity of mood. Those
of Colette's short stories in which "Colette" is the narrator, and they constitute by far the largest group, are
all *nouvelles* in the original sense. Only eighteen of the
twenty-two stories in *La Femme cachée*, five of the
eleven stories in *La Fleur de l'Age*, "Le rendez-vous" in
Bella-Vista, "Armande" in *Le Képi* and "L'Enfant
malade" in *Gigi* [2] are short stories in the current sense
of the term.

The title, *La Femme cachée*, is to some extent mis-
leading, for in these stories it is a question, not only of

the "hidden woman," but also of the "hidden man," unless, of course, the title is to be read as implying that "to hide" is essentially a female trait. It is unsafe to think of the title which Colette gives to a group of stories as applying to them all. Almost always the book takes its name from the first story, but although this is the case in *La Femme cachée*, the word "hidden" is nevertheless pertinent, not only to the theme of all the stories in this particular collection, but to Colette's other short stories as well. In a very unpretentious and concrete manner, Colette is dealing with the problem of reality and appearances.

The differences, as well as the similarities, between Colette's short stories and her novels are striking. On the whole, the short stories are much less subjective. The characters do not fall into the family groups that exist in the novels, nor does the action in which they are involved follow the patterns established in the novels. Of course, as may be expected, most of the short stories deal with aspects of love, but even here there is greater variety in the age, the background and the situation of the characters. In general, too, the men in Colette's short stories are infinitely more sympathetic and stronger than their novelistic counterparts.

The reader will recognize immediately, however, that he is still well within the bounds of Colette's fictional universe. The tendency to move from a particular incident to a general conclusion or implication, the tremendous importance given to a certain kind of detail and, above all, the concision and density of the style reveal the hand and eye of Colette. The short stories, indeed, because of their often minuscule size, are an excellent means to study some of Colette's techniques of composition.

Most of the stories in *La Femme cachée* range from three to four pages in length. Of these, seven are concerned with conjugal love, six with other forms of love, two with the lost paradise of childhood, one with the triumph of life over death as shown in the day of a painter, one with the relation between a woman and her critical butler and one with the semi-crazy people who haunt the offices of daily newspapers.

In each case, the story is a revelation, through an often trivial detail or incident, of what makes people love, fall out of love, go on living, kill, become jealous or heroic. A new hairdo, the constant movement of a thumb over lips, a hand lying on a sheet, a familiar whistle, an anniversary bracelet, an unknown song, a mildewed picture, an omelette, these are some of the seemingly unimportant details from which Colette produces her revelations.

As in the novels, though less often through dialogue, the reader is brought immediately into the action with only the vaguest suggestion of an introductory statement.

"For a long time he had been watching the movement of the masked figures. . . ." [3]
"The surgical suddenness of their rupture left him dumb." [4]
"He had fallen asleep on his young wife's shoulder. . . ." [5]
"He had taken her from another man. . . ." [6]
"When Madame de la Hournerie returned home after a half day entirely consecrated to the hairdresser and the milliner. . . ." [7]
"The access to the little villa was so easy that the robber

wondered why and by what excess of prudence he had waited so long." [8]

"The two young women separated as they had come together, without knowing why." [9]

"When he had killed her, with one stroke of the little lump of lead under which she kept her wrapping paper, Louis became confused." [10]

"The painter who wanted to die made the gesture, at the same time spontaneous and literary, of sketching a few lines before he killed himself." [11]

The factual, undramatic tone of these first sentences, whether they refer to a very ordinary or a very startling situation, sets the mood, and illustrates Colette's very particular, ironic point of view. In using the same tone for all the stories, Colette reduces the extraordinary to the ordinary and raises the ordinary to the extraordinary. Whether the principal character is a murderer, a widow, a bored married man, a newlywed wife, a robber, a Lesbian or a painter on the verge of suicide, becomes of little importance, and this in itself is a sufficient element of surprise to arrest the attention. The contrast between the unconventional status and role of some of the characters and the extreme situations in which some of them are found, and the rather conventional status, role and situation of others, is an all-important key to an understanding of these short stories.

Colette persistently forces acceptance of the fact that there may be no significant difference between the reactions of a perpetually irritated wife and the reactions of an unsuccessful robber. They are both victims of the annoying consequences of their actions, in one case marriage, in the other attempted theft, and they are both capable of a final, heroic silence in which they reveal a

sense of compromise and propriety. Everything and anything human beings do is only a source of small vexa-
tions and small pleasures, which, depending on the angle
of vision, may seem either very unimportant or very
important. Colette is deliberately attempting an anti-
romantic portrayal of human beings. She refuses to over-
dramatize murder, suicide, love, memory, to make of
them anything but "facts." Aside from the very positive
value she gives to silence, Colette is totally unconcerned
with demonstrating anything other than the general notion that all lives are conditioned by details and that
there is no relation between the apparent insignificance
of the detail and the gigantic meaning it may assume as
an instrument of revelation. Just as the novels explore
variations on the theme of love, the short stories explore
variations on the theme of the revealing detail. In the
novels there is essentially one love, and in these short
stories, because of the all-pervading unity of tone, there
is essentially one human being, involved in a variety of
situations, revealed by a variety of details.

In the title story of *La Femme cachée* and in Colette's
longer short stories, the theme of revelation is more fully
developed. Irène in "La Femme cachée," Bernard in "Le
rendez-vous," Armande in "Armande" and Jean in
"L'Enfant malade" reveal themselves as being very different either from the image they attempt to impose on
others (Irène, Armande and Jean) or from the image
they have of themselves (Bernard). Irène, Armande and
Bernard momentarily find a means of escaping from
their false apparent selves to their true selves. Irène, at
a masked ball, protected by her disguise, tastes for an
instant "the monstrous pleasure of being alone, free,

truthful in her native animality, of being the unknown woman, forever solitary and without shame, that a small mask and a hermetic costume have restored to her irremediable solitude and to her dishonest innocence." [12] Armande, ordinarily prudish, becomes loving and caressing in gesture, intimate and vulgar in language, when her timid would-be lover, Maxime, is knocked unconscious by a falling chandelier while leaving her home. Bernard regains a sense of dignity when he helps a wounded Arab boy discovered at the place he and his mistress had chosen for a nocturnal meeting: "Poor Rose. . . . She was my woman, but he is my equal. It is curious that I had to come to Tangiers to meet my equal, the only one who can make me proud of him and proud of me. With a woman, one is easily a little ashamed, of her or of oneself." [13]

Ten-year-old Jean, in "L'Enfant malade," escapes through fever from the real world of his sickbed and the solicitous questions of Madame Maman to a fantastic, poetic world, composed of familiar objects metamorphosed, the existence of which he keeps hidden from those around him. Jean's recovery means the death of this world of perpetual revelation.

In each of these stories, and to a lesser degree in all the short stories of *La Femme cachée* and *La Fleur de l'Age*, the characters are playing a game of hide-and-seek, alone and with others. In general, those who seek find something unexpected, and those who hide are discovered.

Irène's husband, who has deliberately not told his hitherto faithful wife that he is going to the masked ball and who in turn has been similarly deceived, finds her wandering from man to man, taking her fill of kisses. Although she does not recognize him, he recognizes her and allows her to betray herself. Maxime, who has failed miserably in his attempt at controlling his shyness in what he considers to be Armande's forbidding presence, pretends to be unconscious so as to enjoy the revelation of a sensual, affectionate Armande. Bernard, who is prepared for an evening of love, discovers that his mistress is essentially vulgar and that in binding Ahmed's wound with strips torn from his own jacket, he has given and received much more than that which he sought with Rose.

Jean is always beginning to play a game of hide-and-seek with Madame Maman and she with him, but neither of them can be trusted to close his eyes and count to twenty. "She thinks I'm asleep. . . . He thinks that I think he's asleep. . . . She thinks I'm not suffering. . . . How well he knows how to imitate a child who isn't suffering. . . ." [14]

Jean's important game of hide-and-seek is played with death. The further Jean goes in his exploration of a world in which he can fly on a paper knife or ride on a lavender smell, a world in which applesauce is transformed into "an acid young provincial girl of fifteen who, like other girls of the same age, had only disdain and arrogance for the ten-year-old boy," [15] the further he moves from the real world, the closer he comes to death, which is what he is really seeking. Colette refuses Jean what might have been an empty revelation, the very unsatisfactory ending of a dangerous game. She brings him back to a world in which a paper knife cuts, lavender smells and applesauce is an often unattractive food. In abandoning, with Jean, her brief excursion into the world of imaginative revelation, Colette deliberately casts her choice for a world in which revelation is limited to that of the "hidden man" or the "hidden woman."

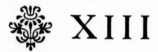

XIII

Playwright and Critic

> *In Balzac's work everything is theater, ex-*
> *cept his theater.*[1]

Colette's astute observation about the theater of Balzac
is equally valid for her own theater. With one comedy,
En Camarades, one *fantaisie lyrique*, *L'Enfant et les Sor-*
tilèges, one *féerie-ballet*, *La Décapitée*, three adaptations
of her own novels, *Chéri*, *La Vagabonde*, *Gigi*, and at
least one adaptation of a foreign play, *Le Ciel de Lit*,[2]
Colette's theater is the least important part, as to both
quantity and quality, of her literary production. Were
it not that her plays reveal, by their very limitations,
certain important aspects of her fictional world, they
might easily be ignored, except for *L'Enfant et les Sorti-*
lèges.

In the composition of her novels and short stories,
Colette, as has been seen, employs many of the techniques of the dramatist. One might suppose this would
augur well for her own plays and adaptations. But

those same dramatic elements that contributed to the success of the novels and short stories—the emphasis on gestures, the rapid dialogue, the brief narrative passages that set and describe the scene of the action, the theme of revelation—are lost on the stage. What becomes evident is that, although Colette does possess some of the technical equipment indispensable to the playwright, her plays are essentially undramatic.

Small dramas, it is true, are the bases of Colette's fictional universe: dramas played out between men and women, between animals and humans, between animals and animals. These, however, are all intimate dramas, in which the revealing gestures, such as the movement of an eyebrow, the dilating of a nostril, cannot possibly pass the footlights except as exaggeration and caricature. These are dramas in which the dramatic tension has its source in the contrast between the very ordinary dialogue of the characters and the description by Colette of their more subtle movements and actions.

In *En Camarades*, Fanchette and Max, a married couple reminiscent of Claudine and Renaud, decide that they shall each do as they please with their private lives. Fanchette is being courted by an adolescent called, very simply, "the kid," and Max is courting Marthe Payet. The do-as-you-please system fails, and Fanchette and Max are reunited in an atmosphere of "togetherness." The moral of the play is, quite clearly, "One should never trifle with love," or, it might be added, with language.

> MAX: Marthe, I must speak seriously with you, I must kiss you, no less seriously.
> MARTHE: Where?

MAX: (impetuously) All over.
MARTHE: (frightened) No! I meant where? in what—
in what place? [3]

Such dialogue is not infrequent in the *Claudine* novels, and *En Camarades* is very close in time to that period of Colette's work. Indeed, Marthe Payet is a character both in the novels and in the play. However, on the stage, Colette cannot suddenly redeem herself by a short descriptive passage, and this play, which in theme and character is very much a part of Colette's fictional world, is an excellent example of the relative unimportance of theme and the extreme importance of how a theme is handled.

Within the form of the novel or the short story, the intellectual inferiority of Colette's characters is counterbalanced by the presence of Colette. Bereft of this presence, obliged to stand alone, supported only by dialogue, the characters tend to become vulgar and banal, and the dramas in which they are involved seem little more than occasionally witty bedroom comedies, a genre that is only too well represented in the French commercial *théâtre du boulevard*.

Because the adaptations of *Chéri*, *La Vagabonde* and *Gigi* were made by Colette in collaboration with someone else, the first two with Léopold Marchand and *Gigi*, with Anita Loos, it is difficult to judge Colette's exact role in the collaboration. In her theater reviews, she often bemoans the fact that the French theater, unlike the English, is traditionally reluctant to mix tragedy and comedy in the same play, and it is quite clear that Colette was attempting to do a great deal of just this in the adaptation of *Chéri*. When her young collaborator remarked that certain words spoken by Léa and Chéri would make the audience laugh and forget Léa's sadness and Chéri's uneasiness, Colette answered, "So they will laugh! What would they do if not consider grotesque what they have just taken seriously and poke fun at their own emotion?" [4] Colette's stated intentions were no doubt sincere, but a comparison of passages in the adaptation and in the novel reveals that she was, above all, attempting to make the audience laugh. The tragic elements are consistently reduced or lost in favor of the comic.

The unfortunate result is that in *Chéri*, the very factor which most contributed to the dramatic atmosphere of the novel, the principals' isolation, as it were, in Léa's sumptuous bedroom, has been abandoned. In the first act of the play, the tête-à-tête between the two main characters is constantly disturbed by the intrusion of visitors. In the last act, the final scene between Léa and Chéri is interrupted by the appearance of Edmée. These intrusions and interruptions do nothing but detract from the dramatic tension.

The passion that unites Léa and Chéri, instead of being, as it was in the novel, implicit and in marked contrast to the tone of much of the dialogue, becomes explicit. "I would have liked to have a child—I know that I have you—but it's not the same thing." [5] This kind of blunt statement, so unlike Colette, is perhaps a sign of the hand of the collaborator. In any case, it is a glaring indication of the inferiority of the play to the novel.

The most successful scenes in the play are those in which Chéri's mother and her decaying friends occupy the center of the stage. In the novel, these characters served both as comic relief and as a means of illuminating the central theme. In the play, which is devoid of any tension that would warrant comic relief, they are simply amusing.

As a play, *La Vagabonde*, like *Chéri*, has lost its most dramatic quality. No allusion is made in the play to the fact that Renée was a writer. Although the prologue reaches further back in time than the novel, to the last day that Renée spends with her husband and his mistresses, Adolphe Taillandy's unseen power is much more convincing as evoked by Renée in the novel than as presented in the opening scenes of the play. Thus, the heart of Renée's conflict, her need for independence, her need to observe for herself, and her terror of falling once more into the sordidness of her first marriage, disappears almost entirely. The play is reduced to a series of pleasant tableaux, many of which incorporate characters and dialogue from *L'Envers du Music-Hall*; *La Vagabonde* is a play in title only.

Gigi is a more successful adaptation, but once again it is inferior to the novel, and the additions in dialogue are heavier, more banal, than the original. Colette and her collaborators seem to have the feeling that the theater is a more vulgar medium than the novel and that to make certain of being fully understood, the playwright must explain all allusions, must leave nothing, or almost nothing, to the spectator's imagination. By a strange reversal, Colette's novels are dramatic and the adaptations episodic.

The sensuous qualities of the novels that are lost in *En Camarades* and in the adaptations reappear in a most exaggerated manner in *La Décapitée*, a scenario for a ballet set to music by Albert Wolff and as yet unproduced. While it was first published in *Mes Cahiers* in 1935, the date of composition of *La Décapitée* is unknown. The story and atmosphere, however, are not unlike those which may be found in the decadent symbolist writings at the end of the nineteenth century.

A sultana is languishing in her tent on the terrace of a palace, awaiting the arrival of her master. Her black, white and yellow servants try to distract her with their dances. The sultana falls asleep and is awakened by the music of a flute. She orders the flute player to be brought before her. The fifteen-year-old nomad, "Grain of Sand," charms her with his flute. They make love on the large, deep cushions. Music announces the arrival of the sultan. Amorously he enters the tent, amorously he caresses his frightened wife, while the flute player, hidden in the cushions, also caresses the sultana. "Grain of Sand" is discovered and killed; the sultana is decapitated. But her headless body returns to torment the sultan with a seductive, lascivious dance. When the sultan attempts to embrace the body, it dissolves, and as he prays that his whole wife be returned to him, a head with an enigmatic smile slowly ascends.

This *féerie-ballet*, as even a brief résumé of the action reveals, is from beginning to end composed of a series of voluptuous, increasingly suggestive movements for which the story is merely the pretext. The rhythm of the language follows that of the action, with short, imperative sentences alternating with long and short poetic stanzas:

THE SLAVE: Humid and of a fire
Which dies neither in the shade
Nor under the sun, take
These scintillating diamonds——

THE SULTANA: (*pushing away the jewels*)
Humid and of a fire
Which dies neither in the shade
Nor under the face of the sun,
I have my eyes.[6]

This deliberately exotic language, combined with the movements, often seems ridiculous. The total effect produced by a reading of *La Décapitée* is similar to that of looking at old pictures of Theda Bara in her most seductive poses. In "Gribiche," a story about a music-hall dancer, Colette speaks of one of the members of the troupe as having played the role of *La Décapitée*. Whether or not Colette's scenario is based on a pre-existent model, there is an obvious relation between the mime dramas in which Colette appeared—*Le Rêve d'Egypte, La Chair, L'Emprise, Le Désir, l'Amour et la Chimère, L'Oiseau de Nuit*—the kind of acting they required, and the overall conception of *La Décapitée*. The play belongs to a very definitely outdated genre. Perhaps Albert Wolff's music transforms *La Décapitée*. Until it is performed, one can at least nourish this illusion.

The most successful of Colette's theatrical endeavors is, beyond all doubt, the libretto for *L'Enfant et les Sortilèges*. Set to music by Maurice Ravel, this *fantaisie lyrique*, aided by an excellent recording, is quite well known both in Europe and America. The most exciting

production to date of *L'Enfant et les Sortilèges* was that
of May, 1939, with choreography by Serge Lifar and
costumes by Paul Colin. It was the last important theatrical presentation in Paris before the beginning of the
second World War.

As in the short story, "L'Enfant malade," the action
in *L'Enfant et les Sortilèges* moves from the real world
to a poetic world and back again to the real. The fact that
in both cases the poetic world is a symptom of disorder
may be taken as an indication of the intensity of Colette's
dedication to the "real."

A little boy in a bad mood refuses to do his homework,
sticks his tongue out at his mother, breaks the teapot and
the teacup, wounds the squirrel with a knife, pulls the
cat's tail, pours water on the fire, tears at the wallpaper
with a poker, takes the clock apart, mutilates his books
and then, drunk with destructiveness, shouting, "Hur-
rah!" starts to sit down on an armchair, which calmly
hops away like a frog.

By his intentional meanness, the little boy has destroyed the normal order of things within his own small
universe. "Imprudent little barbarian," says the fire,
"you insulted all the benevolent gods who raised a fragile
barrier between you and misfortune." [7] To our delight
and to the child's terror, the armchair dances with an
eighteenth-century easy chair; the clock sings and
walks; the Wedgwood teapot speaks in English to the
Chinese teacup which answers in Chinese or a reason-
able facsimile; the shepherds, the shepherdesses, the
sheep, a dog, and a goat bid each other farewell and
bewail their lost existence in the wallpaper world; the
story-book princess is seized by the malevolent powers

of Sleep and Night; and Arithmetic, in the form of a
wizened old man, dances around the little boy in a sin-
ister manner, incorrectly shouting the multiplication
table. After the tumult created by the broken and torn
objects has reached its peak and died away, it is the
turn of the injured animals and trees of the garden to
torment, bewilder and frighten the little boy. The trees
complain of their knife marks; the dragonfly and the
bat demand the return of their companions; the squirrel
harangues the child for having taken away his liberty
by putting him in a cage.

More and more animals come into the garden, play
with each other, caress each other and ignore the child.
"Maman," cries the little boy, and suddenly aware of
his presence, all the animals fly at him, jump at him,
push him, pull him. The wounded little boy and a
wounded squirrel are hurled into a corner. The little
boy binds the squirrel's wounds, and the other animals,
quick to forgive, carry the child to his mother. The little
boy broke the wicked spell by his single act of kindness.
The normal order of his world is reestablished.

The repeated half words, half sentences, whole sentences, the rhythmical, occasionally rhymed stanzas, are
deliberate and successful attempts at reproducing the
patterns of incantations. The libretto is thus composed
of verbal charms, which create an atmosphere of total
enchantment. Says the Wedgwood teapot to the little
boy in a jumble of French and English:

> Black and costaud
> Black and chic and jolly fellow
> I punch, sir, I punch your nose
> I knock you out, stupid chose!

Black, and chic, and vrai beau gosse,
I box you, I marm'lad you.[8]

Says the wizened old man:

Millimeter
Centimeter
Decimeter
Decameter
Hectometer
Kilometer
Myriameter
Billions
Trillions
Frac-cillions.[9]

Say all the animals and the trees:

It's the child with the knife!
It's the child with the stick!
The bad boy with the cage!
The bad boy with the net!
He who likes no one
And whom no one likes!
Shall we flee?
No! we shall punish.
I have my claws!
I have my teeth!
I have my wings!
Unite, Unite! [10]

Nowhere else in Colette's works written for the stage
was she able to maintain both dramatic action and poetic language. It is in the realm of fantasy, at the point
furthest removed from her novels, that Colette, though
only once and in the shortest possible form, conquered at
least some of the difficulties of the theater.

Colette's most valuable contribution to the theater is not, however, *L'Enfant et les Sortilèges*, but the reviews which she wrote for various Parisian newspapers from October 8, 1933, to June 5, 1938. Collected under the title *La Jumelle noire*, these reviews fill an entire volume of the *Oeuvres complètes*.

"The duty of affirming an opinion spoils a great number of our joys," writes Colette in the preface to *La Jumelle noire*, reiterating her often-expressed distaste for the task of the critic. Despite this distaste, Colette, with or without her black opera glasses to aid her myopic eyes and increase her "malice," as she puts it, faithfully attended the dress rehearsals and the premières in the Parisian theaters and once a week wrote a review of one, two, sometimes three or four plays.

Colette was indeed, as she says in the preface, an "indulgent critic." Her own experience in the music hall and her knowledge of the difficulty of writing well tended to make her find something pleasant to say about almost everything. This attitude did not prevent her making occasional derisive remarks about an actor or a playwright, and rendering her likes and dislikes abundantly clear (she heartily disliked Shakespeare's pastoral plays, Molière's *Georges Dandin* and Dumas' *La Dame aux Camélias*), but it did prevent her adopting the superior tone common to many drama critics who have never themselves been either creative writers or actors.

From 1933 to 1938 the avant-garde theater was at its height in France under the direction of Copeau, Dullin, Pitoëff, Baty and Jouvet. Their revolutionary methods of directing, staging and acting a play, their reinterpretations of classics, their receptivity to new forms of drama, such as the plays of Pirandello, Cocteau, Giraudoux, Anouilh, Salacrou, won for them the acclaim of intellectual audiences throughout Europe. But the theater that flourished financially in these years was the commercial *théâtre du boulevard*. The sophisticated plays of Sacha Guitry, the social plays of Edouard Bourdet and the psychological plays of Henry Bernstein, all of which were to appear dated after the second World War, were the popular box-office successes of the 1933–1938 period.

Colette was not a member of the literary avant-garde. She is obviously more at home in discussing the complexities of a drama dealing with adultery than she is in discussing Dullin's interpretation of Shakespeare's *Richard III* or Antonin Artaud's first experiment with a *théâtre de la cruauté, Les Cenci*. Although she admires the dedication and the brilliance of the "Cartel"—Dullin, Pitoëff, Baty and Jouvet—and other innovators, Colette almost always finds their productions "excessive." Her general conception of the theater is that of the regular theater-goer, the intelligent bourgeois for whom the theater means essentially a well-written, well-performed drama, and who, at the end of a performance, is usually more interested in what the author had to say about love or death than how he said it or how the director projected it.

If Colette at times seems inadequate in her intellectual understanding of the most interesting theatrical efforts of these years, she never fails in her appreciation of the best plays and the best actors. The two plays which evoked her unbounded enthusiasm were Giraudoux's *La Guerre de Troie n'aura pas lieu*, and Cocteau's

La Machine infernale, and the young actors whose success she immediately predicted were Claude Dauphin, Jean-Louis Barrault and Jacques Tati.

Colette saw bad, mediocre and good plays. Since her articles had always to be of a certain length, the bad and the mediocre received as much attention as the good. But one does not read Colette's articles merely to find out whether she thought a play was good or bad, and how taste has or has not changed in twenty years. To read *La Jumelle noire* is to recapture the atmosphere of a certain period and is still another means of entering into the world of Colette.

The reviews follow a similar pattern: an introductory section, usually chatty in nature and indicating Colette's approval or disapproval, an often lengthy résumé of the play and a final evaluation of the actors' performances. Sometimes, in discussing a particular play, Colette combines the talents of the prose writer and the memorialist and re-creates an entire evening at the theater: the audience, the seats, the play, the lighting, the sets, the performers, remarks overheard during intermissions, everything that contributes toward an ephemeral experience has been preserved by Colette's reviews, which satisfy both the casual reader and the student of the theater.

As may be expected, Colette triumphs in her articles on the music hall and the flamboyant spectacles at the Casino de Paris or the Folies Bergères. This is the theatrical world which Colette knows and loves best. The colors, the costumes, the bodies of the women, the appeal of the star—Mistinguett, Maurice Chevalier, Cécile Sorrel, Josephine Baker—the excitement of the audience, these

Colette describes with the same punctilious attention to detail as in her novels and short stories.

The outstanding quality of Colette's reviews is that they are extremely well written and extremely personal:

> A great and final modesty under our display of cynicism and beyond our familiarity with incest and homosexuality, or rather a great repugnance, restrains us from mixing, as does life, the comic and the sensuous, burlesque and emotion.[11]

> In art, inhumanity does not constitute a deficiency.[12]

> Boredom at least has its bitterness and leaves its trace on my lips. But what is an evening at the theater that liberates at midnight an uncertain crowd, not angry to have sounded the depths of the soft, the predictable, the facile, stuffed with commonplaces, with sweetish aphorisms and with what ease, with what lightness— Neither angry nor even bored, because Monsieur Pujol does not lack skill, is not maladroit.[13]

The first sentence sums up and explains an entire aspect of the so-called "Gallic" theater; the aphorism postulates an essential difference between the morality of life and the morality of art; the description of a lost evening at the theater is both an analysis of emptiness and a gently devastating piece of criticism. There are, of course, less good passages in the reviews, over-florid descriptions and an occasionally banal aphorism. In general, however, despite the fact that the reviews were of necessity hastily written, the vocabulary retains the same precision, the sentences the same poetic rhythm, as in Colette's most scrupulously composed fiction.

Colette always is "Colette." Not even as drama critic does she forget Sido, Saint-Sauveur-en-Puisaye, cats, the

problem of growing old, her love of long hair, her pref-
erence for ample, well-fed women, her admiration for
Balzac, her interest in children, her devotion to the
color blue, her dissatisfaction with the atheistic and
Catholic conceptions of death. An article by Colette
tends to take the form of an anecdote written in the
first person in which the main character is Colette herself. Suspect as this procedure may be in a drama critic,
it was what charmed the contemporary reader and
what continues to charm. It is the procedure that characterizes the largest and most significant part of her
literary work. Colette's real drama is the drama of her
personal relation to the world.

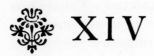 # XIV

Anecdote and Meditation: Daily Adventures

> *To choose, to note the conspicuous, to preserve the unusual, to eliminate the banal, is not my concern, since, almost always, it is the ordinary that excites and animates me.*[1]

Thirty-three of the fifty-seven titles included in the *Oeuvres complètes* are works written in the first person. Both in quantity and in quality these works, originally written as newspaper chronicles or as short stories and articles for different anthologies or as advertisements or as single books, dominate Colette's literary production. Although they treat a wide variety of subjects—animals, plants, music halls, Sido, childhood, fashion, Willy, travels, old age, love in all possible forms, Parisian events, famous writers and murderers, Colette's daughter, Bel-Gazou, France—and although the manner of presentation may be an anecdote, a dialogue, a description, a short or long meditation, Colette's first-person writings are of interest essentially as the expression of a relation between the narrator, "Colette," and the world.

These first-person writings are neither diaries nor intimate journals. With the exception of *Mes Apprentissages*, they tell nothing, or very little, of Colette's private affairs. They reveal, not a life, but a style of living and a style of writing. The reader's intimacy with Colette is both real and illusory. In the aesthetic distance that separates Colette from "Colette," the real woman is transformed into a fictional character who, drawing on the memories and the experiences of the original model, becomes the distinctive voice that rules a charmed but very real domain.

This voice is first heard in *Les Vrilles de la Vigne*. Published in 1908,[2] *Les Vrilles de la Vigne* contains the same major themes as those that were elaborated in the *Claudine* novels: childhood, nature, love and solitude. But the treatment of these themes takes a new form, and the atmosphere in which they are developed changes. Colette has put aside the fictional universe she created in her first novels in favor of brief chapters sustained and unified by a single voice.

Thus, at the beginning of her independent literary career, when Colette took off the mask and wrote in her own name, she did not choose the novel as her vehicle of expression. The *Dialogues de Bêtes*, the last pages of *La Retraite sentimentale* and *Les Vrilles de la Vigne* clearly show that Colette, left to herself, tended toward poetic revery and anecdote rather than toward fiction. This change from fiction to revery, from Claudine to "Colette," is accompanied by a movement away from the adult human world to the world of memory and the world of animals. The importance accorded to memory and animals in these early independent works, the need to communicate in relative solitude both with the past and with elemental, primitive forces, is indicative of Colette's withdrawal from the human world as she had transposed it in the *Claudine* series and experienced it in the years spent with Monsieur Willy.

Many of Colette's first-person writings follow this same pattern of withdrawal. In her novels, Colette creates characters involved in situations which reflect certain of her own experiences, temptations and premonitions. In her first-person writings, she creates a character who, free from the conventions of plot and action, reveals, as it were, the fruits of these involvements, in a commentary on life as seen by one who has temporarily withdrawn from it. The freedom, both in content and expression, to be found in such works as *Les Vrilles de la Vigne*, counterbalances the controlled rigidity of many of the novels and short stories and serves to illuminate the characters and situations created in these more conventional works.

Both in matter and in manner *Les Vrilles de la Vigne* anticipates the entire range of Colette's first-person writings. It stands in much the same relation to these writings as do the *Claudines* to the later novels. *Les Vrilles de la Vigne* establishes a general pattern, a pattern on which, in her first-person works, she elaborates but from which she never deviates.

The book thus marks a point of arrival and a point of departure. It takes its title from the lyrical opening pages, among the most beautiful that Colette ever wrote. In "Les Vrilles de la Vigne," she describes a nightingale who is caught while sleeping one night by the tendrils of the vine and who thereafter sings in order to keep awake, eventually becoming enchanted with its own voice. Through the image of the nightingale, Colette symbolically portrays her childhood, her first marriage and the liberation that came with the discovery of her talent. Writing, Colette implies, has become for her, as singing for the nightingale, a mode of life, the necessary element for survival.

Colette reveals the quality of her voice to herself and to the reader in these opening pages, and she introduces a first-person narrator, "Colette," whose desire it is to write "Everything that I know, everything that I think, everything that I divine, everything that enchants me and wounds me and astonishes me," [3] and who thereby heralds the advent of all that part of Colette's work which falls under the heading of meditations and reminiscences: *La Naissance du Jour, Mes Apprentissages, Le Pur et l'Impur, De ma Fenêtre, Trois . . . Six . . . Neuf . . ., Belles Saisons, L'Etoile Vesper* and *Le Fanal bleu.*

As is the case with *Les Vrilles de la Vigne,* the titles of these meditations and reminiscences are all symbolic and mark different stages of Colette's life and development. *La Naissance du Jour* symbolizes the birth of a new attitude toward life, a new renunciation and a new acceptance. *Mes Apprentissages* evokes the years of apprenticeship, both as a writer and as a woman, which Colette spent with Monsieur Willy. *Le Pure et l'Impur* indicates her refusal to accept conventional morality. *De ma*

Fenêtre portrays her immobility, her arthritis, which, forcing her to stay in bed, permits her to see and to live in only that part of the world which is visible from her window. *Trois . . . Six . . . Neuf . . .*[4] refers to Colette's unwelcome, yet ever-increasing changes of residence. *Belles Saisons* calls up the eternal beauty of the natural world for one who is forced to live mostly in memory. *L'Etoile Vesper* symbolizes Colette's decline. *Le Fanal bleu* describes the narrowing of her world to those objects which are illuminated by an electric light bulb, shaded by a piece of blue paper. The light of the *fanal bleu* in Colette's window announces to the world that she is, despite her illness and her great age, still alive.

As Colette grows older, the autobiographical elements in these meditations and reminiscences increase. "Novels, short stories, embellished episodes, skilful arrangements of fiction and truth, I managed to do all this. But now the difficulty of walking and the years put me in a situation where I no longer sin by lying and banish from me all occasions for flights of fancy."[5] The Colette who can be known most fully, therefore, is the ailing, arthritic Colette of *L'Etoile Vesper* and *Le Fanal bleu*. A series of masks and models have been discarded, until finally, just before death, the character and the woman meet.

These works vary in quality but not in kind. A flower, an evening wind, people reading in the park, one of Sido's letters and Colette starts off on a path that leads from the present to the past and back again to the present, recalling the voices of friends, the color of the sea, a summer in Provence, an incident from her childhood, combining these with the hardships of war, the pains of arthritis, an unexpected visit, a short conversation with her faithful companion.

A rambling promenade of this sort, even in the company of Colette, may become tedious, but this tedium is the ransom required to redeem from captivity, the captivity of laziness and habit, one's own attentiveness to detail, one's own often dormant senses. Colette compels her readers to look, to smell, to taste, to touch, to hear. She forces them into a new and intimate relation with living things and with objects. And as there is no sudden illumination in Colette's world, tedium is the prerequisite of wisdom. Colette the moralist is ever present in Colette the sensualist, drawing from the smallest detail a lesson, and always the same lesson, that lucidity is more precious than happiness and that lucidity demands constant vigilance.

"Nuit Blanche," "Jour Gris" and "Le Dernier Feu," the three lyrical monologues in *Les Vrilles de la Vigne*, are short poems in prose, rhapsodic evocations of mood and landscape. In "Nuit Blanche," the narrator, beginning with a description of "our bed," proceeds to tell of a night of insomnia during which the memory of a garden is linked with the memory of love and of pleasure. "You gave me flowers without thorns. . . ."[6] At the end of a rather audacious evocation of Sapphic caresses, there is a concluding sentence which foreshadows and perhaps explains the origin of the relationship between Léa and Chéri: "You will give me pleasure, bent over me, your eyes full of maternal anxiety, you, who are seeking in your passionate friend the child you never had." [7]

In "Jour Gris" and "Le Dernier Feu," the narrator speaks to her anonymous though clearly feminine lover, contrasting the maritime country in which they are with the country of her childhood. Perhaps the most striking note in these monologues is that of melancholy, a melancholy which is always associated, in Colette's world, with love. Here the melancholy is a result both of physical love and of the loss of the narrator's "true" love, her childhood. The juxtaposition of childhood and homosexuality is not fortuitous. As shall be seen later, in a discussion of Colette's "masterpieces," the link lies in the word "pure."

The three chapters in *Les Vrilles de la Vigne* which compose the "Valentine" cycle are forerunners of Colette's longer first-person short stories: "Bella-Vista" in *Bella-Vista*, "Chambre d'hôtel" and "La lune de pluie" in *Chambre d'Hôtel*, "Le Képi" and "Le Tendron" in *Le Képi* and "La Dame du Photographe" in *Gigi*.

> It is insane to think that the periods without love are "empty spaces" in a woman's existence. On the contrary. . . . These "empty spaces" which took it upon themselves to furnish me with anecdotes, with troubled, lost, incomprehensible or simple characters who tugged at my sleeve, used me as witness, then let me go, I did not know then that they were more romantic interludes than my own personal dramas.[8]

Colette spent these "periods without love" in Paris or in French provincial hotels. The "romantic interludes" are transformed into short stories in which Colette appears as narrator, observer and character. Ostensibly these are "real" stories, based on real anecdotes, about people whom Colette meets in her travels; sometimes, as in the "Valentine" stories, "Le Képi" and "Le Tendron," real friends supposedly tell Colette their past or present experiences. The air of authenticity is reinforced by the presence of other real people: Willy, Georges Wague, Annie de Pène, Paul Masson.

The atmosphere in these stories is always mysterious. What is Valentine's "disguised sorrow"? What is the connection between Monsieur Daste and the dead birds? What is Madame Ruby? Why does Monsieur Haume never stop looking at his watch? What is the strange relation between Colette's past and the two sisters who live in her old apartment? Why does the photographer's wife attempt to kill herself? Why does Albin Chaveriat, at the age of seventy, refuse the invitation of a friend whose household abounds in young girls?

Colette would have one believe that the people whose stories she narrates are all ordinary people, each possessed of a particular secret, living a particular drama, a drama that would have passed unnoticed were it not for the writer who, observing the tics and the habits of her habitual or chance acquaintances, divines, intuits, imagines and creates. If one were to protest that a person such as Madame Ruby, supposedly a Lesbian but really a man, or the series of coincidences that bring together the characters in "Chambre d'hôtel" hardly seem ordinary, Colette would undoubtedly answer that the protest reveals inability to see, that everyone does have a secret, that everyone, at some time, is caught in a web of coincidences. Colette never fails to use such phrases as "the lover of young girls," or "the betrayed lover," or "the spinster," thereby implying that her characters belong to, and behave in a manner appropriate to, a general class of humanity.

That "Colette" attracts confidences and confessions, there can be no doubt. Her name is known even to chance acquaintances, and as she is a willing card player and a good listener, it is not very difficult to engage her socially. What is most revealing about "Colette" is that she is quite obviously unable to bear the solitude for which she pretends to yearn. Her arrival at a hotel is followed by a period of uneasiness caused by the strangeness of her room, the difference in the air and the necessity of speaking to unknown people. Her one desire is to return immediately to Paris. And yet, although she frequently reiterates that her acquaintances and their problems bore or annoy her, that she prefers the company of her dog or her cat to human contacts, once the initial presentations have been made, "Colette" quite willingly plays the role of detective or accomplice and soon finds that her room is livable, the air refreshing and the people interesting.

Her fear of solitude, a strong curiosity and a very real affection for human beings, an affection which "Colette" is often reluctant to admit, invariably propel her toward others. But it is not merely by chance that the secrets she discovers, the dramas in which she becomes entangled, reflect her own secrets, her own private dramas, that the "real" first-person short stories should bear so strong a resemblance to the invented third-person short stories. The "real" world of her experiences and her created world are very much the same. The only im-

portant difference between the two is that in the "real"
world the revelation is double. A mystery is resolved,
and "Colette" is partially unmasked. The moral of the
story, and there is always a moral, supports the double
revelation and becomes an apology for the drama, its
actors and its narrator.

> Whenever I think of her, I always see her firmly en-
> trenched behind scruples that she modestly called annoy-
> ances and sustained by outbursts of feminine grandeur,
> humble and everyday, a grandeur which she misjudged by
> inflicting on it the name of "a very small life." [9]

The women, of which "my friend Valentine" is the first,
are the unsuspecting heroines of Colette's first-person
short stories. They are always courageous and always
unaware of their courage, which, were it not for Colette,
would have passed unnoticed. Colette lifts these women
from oblivion, demonstrating once more that drama and
heroism, far from being exceptions, are integral parts of
many a "very small life."

The narrator, "Colette," also shares in this "feminine
grandeur, humble and everyday." Her own daily life,
her own "scruples," which she, too, modestly calls "annoyances," constitute in fact the second, complementary
drama in these stories, a drama which she pretends to
ignore. This lonely woman, so ready to apply the adjective "courageous" to others—is she not, by implication,
the most courageous of all and her stories the proof of
this courage that grapples with the daily adventure, attempting to give it a meaning and a value?

Aside from the very specific nature of the subject matter, "Music-Halls" in *Les Vrilles de la Vigne* and Co-

lette's later music-hall anecdotes, *L'Envers du Music-Hall* and "Gribiche" in *Bella-Vista*, belong with the first-person short stories. In the music hall as in her chance acquaintanceships, "Colette" is both an outsider and a participant, more conscious of the task of illuminating the life of her companions than of the fact that she is revealing her own. Colette's music-hall stories are documents on a world that no longer exists, sentimental tales in which the moral twist often seems excessive. One begins to wonder whether poverty and hard work are always attributes of heroism and dignity, whether intellectual mediocrity always implies moral superiority and whether Colette is not relying a little too much on her own facility to move from the particular to the general.

It is in the light of Colette's pre-music-hall existence, her life with Monsieur Willy, that this emphasis on pride, dignity and morality is brought into proper focus. If it weakens the anecdotes, it nevertheless strengthened Colette. The music-hall stories, for all their local color, are essentially studies in the development of the character "Colette."

The diversity of such chapters in *Les Vrilles de la Vigne* as "La Dame qui chante," "Le Miroir," "En Baie de somme" and "Partie de pêche" is characteristic of the varied chronicles and often unrelated anecdotes that fill the pages of such works as *Dans la Foule, Les Heures longues, La Chambre éclairée, Le Voyage égoïste, Aventures quotidiennes, Journal à rebours, Mes Cahiers, Trait pour Trait, Journal intermittent, La Fleur de l'Age, En Pays connu, A Portée de la main* and *Mélanges*.

Colette could and indeed did write about anything and everything that came within the range of her own daily adventures. There is not one of her voyages, not one of the well-known people she met, not one of the sections of Paris in which she lived, hardly a succulent meal eaten, a change in women's styles, a child encountered, that is not carefully and faithfully transcribed. Colette achieved a major triumph in bringing into the body of literature a very unusual record of the peoples, places and things observed, in a long lifetime, by one woman. But the subject that dominates *Les Vrilles de la Vigne*, the subject to which Colette devoted many pages in the works cited above, not to mention one novel, *La Chatte*, and six short books, *Dialogues de Bêtes*, *La Paix chez les Bêtes*, *Autres Bêtes*, *Prisons et Paradis*, *Flore et Pomone* and *Pour un Herbier*, the subject which, along with love and childhood, obviously stands highest in her favor, is that of the animal and vegetable kingdoms. Even more perhaps than her relations with human beings and human events, Colette's contacts with flora and fauna reveal the limits and the depths of her anecdotes and meditations.

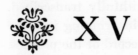 **XV**

Cats and Orchids

"There is only one animal! Do you understand, Maurice, there is only one animal!" [1]

It is not sufficient to say that she loved animals. Before all manifestations of animal or vegetable life, she felt a respect which resembled religious fervor. At the same time, she deeply sensed the unity of creation in the infinite diversity of forms. [2]

In the many anecdotal and biographical sketches written about Colette by her close friends and acquaintances, there is one point of unanimous agreement. Whenever Colette, in the country or on a street or in someone's home, encountered an animal, there was an immediate and evident mutual attraction. Not only that, there was an almost uncanny appearance of communication. For this instinctive rapport, no logical explanation seems possible.

"I cannot remain for a long time without speaking of animals," [3] writes Colette in *De ma Fenêtre*, and the role allotted to them in her writings, from the first page of *Claudine à l'Ecole* to the last pages of *En Pays connu*, attests to the validity of this statement. In the rich animal literature of France, from the anonymous twelfth-century fables to Guillaume Apollinaire's *Bestiaire ou Cortège d'Orphée*, Colette occupies a very special place. Her originality is that she attempts to portray, not only a particular species, but within the species an individual animal which she knows.[4] Unlike most writers of animal tales, Colette has no intention of depicting the foibles of human beings through descriptions of animal behavior, but rather, like Jean de La Fontaine, means to show the resemblance among all living things.

Colette's need to be surrounded by flowers and animals is a deep, sensuous need, the need to caress, to touch fur and petals. In *Claudine en Ménage*, Claudine both bemoans and to a certain degree explains her very particular sensuality. "*Hélas!* How the sight of what I love, the beauty of my friend, the fragrance of the forests, the desire for Renaud, arouses in me the same emotion, the same hunger for possession and embraces! . . . Have I only one mode of feeling?"[5] It would seem that for Colette, as for her character, Claudine, to whom in this respect she is very close, there is only "one mode of feeling" and that is why there is only "one animal." Male, female, animal and flower are "one" because of Colette's physical reaction to them. They are all possible objects of her desire and her joy.

Flowers and animals are associated in Colette's mind with Sido, and are therefore imbued with the magic and beauty of childhood. This association is fully expressed when the sixteen-year-old narrator in "Ma Mère et les

Bêtes" returns home after a two-week sojourn in Paris. "As if I were discovering them together, I greeted at the same time my mother, the garden and the circle of animals." [6] Like Sido, Colette not only rejoices in the daily spectacles provided by animals, she learns from them and lives for them. Colette relates that Sido, in enumerating the hidden riches of her garden, forgot what she had planted in one particular spot and demanded that her young daughter promise not to dig out of curiosity.

> She knew that I should be unable to resist, any more than she, the desire to know, and that following her example, I should rummage in the earth of the flowerpot until it disclosed its secret. Although I never thought of our resemblance, she knew that I was her daughter and that, even though a child, I was already seeking for that shock, that accelerated beating of the heart, that stoppage of breath: the solitary frenzy of the treasure-seeker. [7]

To Sido's reverence for natural phenomena, Colette adds a restrained pessimism in regard to the human world and human contacts which makes the animal world and animal contacts even more attractive. Animals and flowers cannot hurt or deceive Colette as do human beings. However, animals, particularly wild animals, often suffer because of man. Colette tends to associate herself with the suffering animal; she, too, is a free spirit who has been betrayed and trapped but who, like the animals she speaks of in "Le Coeur des Bêtes," [8] attempts to have confidence in man despite his crimes.

Cats and dogs appear most frequently among Colette's animal creations, and they are followed by other household and garden creatures, birds, spiders and butterflies, and, of course, by the flowers of France. If cats and dogs occupy a privileged place in this animal hierarchy it is because, more than their four-legged, many-legged or winged brethren, they have so often entered into a relationship with human beings.

Even when Colette is not directly concerned with flora and fauna they are present in her works. Colette uses the animal and plant kingdoms as a constant source of analogies for her human creations.[9] Indeed, if Colette's human characters are often described in vegetal or animal terms, her non-human characters receive a very human treatment on a psychological plane. Human beings often resemble animals and animals often behave like human beings. The line that separates the human and animal worlds in Colette's work is sometimes so fine as to be almost indiscernible. This is particularly true where cats are concerned. Colette not only prefers cats to other animals; at times, she even prefers them to human beings. "Belle Fanchette," says Claudine to her cat, "how interesting and understanding you are! (much more so than Luce Lanthenay, that inferior cat)."[10] And when Colette is forced to abandon her tiger cat, Bâ-tou, because of Bâ-tou's innocent and natural, but ferocious behavior, she writes, "When I miss you, Bâ-tou, I add to my sorrow the mortification of having chased from my home a friend, a friend who, thank God, had nothing in common with humans."[11] "In frequenting cats," says Colette in "Amours," deliberately implying a contrast with human contacts, "one can only be enriched."[12] And a little further on in the same chapter she comments, "Yes, in my life there were many dogs—but there was the cat. I am indebted to the cat species for an honorable kind of dissimulation, a mastery over myself, a marked aversion for brutal sounds and the need to be silent for a long time." [13]

Many of the moral "recipes" in such works as *La Naissance du Jour*, *L'Etoile Vesper* and *Le Fanal bleu* originate in Colette's observations of feline love and feline suffering. Colette's insistence on bearing pain in silence, on accepting the inevitable, her need for order and freedom, are traits common to the cats she describes. Colette herself, like so many children, grew up under the sign of the cat. Sido's favorite name for her daughter was *Minet-Chéri*; the English equivalent for *minet* is kitten.

It is in the novel *La Chatte* that Colette most explicitly suggests the superiority of the cat and most completely explores the depth of animal feeling and its relation to human feeling. Saha, the cat, not only gives the novel its title, but she is the major and most convincing character in it.

In *La Chatte*, as in all her better novels, Colette is telling a love story and something else. The love story concerns Camille, Alain and Saha; the "something else" is the problem of communication. Camille and Alain, both products of a Parisian bourgeoisie, are married. Camille is an attractive, ordinary young woman; Alain is a daydreaming, sensitive young man, very fond of his mother, his garden and his cat. Saha, for both Alain and Colette, is a source of infinite animal analogies. She is described as having "a long spine softer than a hare's fur." [14] Alain calls her "My little bear with big cheeks. . . . My blue pigeon." [15] Saha climbing up the wall is described as imitating "the gray lizard, flattened against the wall with her paws spread out." [16] Saha during the day "knew how to change herself into a turbulent dog." [17] Saha walks "with a long doe-like step." [18] Saha, chasing a mole, "scratched like a fox terrier, rolled over like a lizard, jumped on all four paws like a frog, clutched a ball of earth between her thighs as a field mouse does the egg he has stolen." [19] But for Alain, even more important than her charming ways, are Saha's moral qualities—"her infinite disinterestedness, her knowledge of how to live, her affinities with a human elite." [20]

Saha and Alain too, one must suppose, belong to this elite, an elite from which Alain's wife, Camille, with her bourgeois vulgarity, her loud voice, her knack for being either over- or under-dressed, is most definitely excluded. Only once does Camille come near to Alain's feline ideal; it is the second time Alain makes love to his wife. "She was lying against him, her arms and legs relaxed, her hands half closed, and feline for the first time." [21] But immediately Alain wonders, "Where is Saha?" and Camille is again relegated to that impure human world in which Alain refuses to live.

Saha becomes for Alain a symbol of love, purity and understanding and for Camille a focus of hatred and jealousy. Shocked by his young wife's lack of modesty, by the rapidity with which the first night of marriage changes her from a virgin into a voracious lover, Alain turns more and more away from her and more and more toward his cat. Between Alain and Saha exists a subtle and mysterious world of correspondences and comprehension which is expressed through Saha's purrs and gestures, Alain's words and gestures. Theirs is the perfect, ideal love affair, based on a mutual need and understanding, unsullied by the demands of physical love. Saha is for Alain everything that Camille is not. It is through Alain's and Camille's reactions to her that the reader sees Saha, and it is, in turn, through Saha, that Alain and Camille are revealed.

As in most of Colette's novels, the main setting of *La Chatte* is a small apartment. The tension within this strange trio grows, and the explosion finally comes when Camille, in a fit of jealous rage, pushes Saha off the balustrade of the terrace. Alain discovers the deed and the culprit and, accompanied by a frightened but alive Saha, leaves his wife.

What is most startling in this novel is not Alain's love for Saha, but Saha's love for Alain and the relationship thereby established between them. Saha refuses to eat, she pines away during the first week of Alain's marriage, and when she is brought into the newlyweds' small apartment, her jealousy of Camille is immediately evident. Saha is physically a cat, a beautiful cat. She expresses herself in sound and movement like a cat. But it is only Saha's physical being that differentiates her from the two other important characters in the novel. And given a scale of human values on which the capacity to love, to feel and to understand is near the top, Saha is more human than Camille.

It is here, more than in any other work, that Colette most clearly reveals her limitation and her originality. Colette's refusal to recognize, to accept or even to consider the world through any abstract form of reference is complete; it imposes restrictions on her work, but it is not without advantages. Insofar as is humanly possible, there exists between Colette and the outer world no screen, no preconceived plan. Colette does not adhere to any a priori metaphysical or moral system of thought. She is therefore open and accessible, within her own limits, to all manifestations of life. All observable life receives equal attention from her senses and her pen. In this universe, in which the greatest good would seem to be equivalent to the greatest intensity of feeling, in which living beings are judged, not by their actions, which may be governed by conscious thought, but by their capacity to live fully, there is no reason why a cat cannot surpass a woman.

Colette's originality lies in the fact that she has neither reduced the human to the animal nor raised the animal to the human; she merely seems not to make the very ordinary distinction between the two. There is only "one animal" for Colette, be it on two legs or four. There are differences, to be sure, but these differences fade before the great common denominator which is life. And so it is possible for a man and a cat to come together in that rather hazy realm in which all living things are one.

The *Dialogues de Bêtes* was the first work Colette wrote under her own name. Disappointed and deceived by the human world that Monsieur Willy and his cohorts represented, unhampered by her husband's proddings, Colette turned to her companions in solitude. "I was vaguely awakening to a duty toward myself, a duty to write something other than the *Claudines*. And drop by drop I exuded the *Dialogues de Bêtes*, in which I gave myself the honorable, if not the lively pleasure of not speaking of love." [22] In the *Dialogues de Bêtes* the animals, a cat, Kiki-la-Doucette, and a dog, Toby-Chien,

speak to each other and to themselves. These animals
not only comment on their own world, they comment
also, as spectators, on the human comedy. Through their
rather precious speeches, through the small scenes and
dramas in which they are involved, they show their uncanny understanding of the human beings they live
with, of *Elle* and of *Lui*.[23]

Toby-Chien is simple, good, honest and humble; Kiki-
la-Doucette is an independent, proud, subtle, egotistical
animal, forever harking back to that time when she and
those of her race were gods. Despite the fact that these
two speak a highly literary language, that their thoughts
are inevitably human, they nevertheless remain animals, they retain the style of their species. Despite the
anthropomorphism, Toby is always canine and Kiki is
always feline, and, what is even more remarkable,
Toby is an individual dog called Toby, as Kiki is an individual cat called Kiki. They cannot be confused with
other cats or dogs in Colette's animal writings. If these
extremely literate animals—more literate, more specula-
tive, in fact, than any of Colette's other characters aside
from "Sido" and herself—retain their respective canine
and feline qualities, as well as their own personalities,
it is due to the manner in which they are described, the
poetic detail which surrounds them.

Each of the dialogues is preceded by a short paragraph which sets the stage for the action. The reader is
given the place, "the steps in full sun," "a bedroom in
the country," "a living room in the country," and usually the time, "the after-lunch siesta," "the end of a
summer's day," "a winter afternoon in Paris." There is
also a short description of the physical condition of Kiki-

la-Doucette and Toby-Chien. The very articulate conversations in which these two domestic animals become involved always have their source in the physical world, and it is this more than any other single factor which allows the animals to remain animals, and which permits the reader to accept their flowery speech. Toby tormented by flies, Toby overstuffed with food, Toby sleeping badly or Kiki locked in a basket, Kiki in front of the fire, Kiki washing herself are very normal states of animal being which Colette, with her usual precision, minutely describes. The step from sensation to thought is a big one, but Colette takes the step with such apparent ease that the reader follows her. A dialogue is always possible, since Colette never for a moment forgets either the traditional antagonism between cat and dog or the traditional rivalry between two household pets.

It is the mixture of real and unreal, of exact description and poetic language, which renders these dialogues believable. One is asked only to accept a poetic truth.

In Colette's succeeding animal stories, the animals do not always speak. They are presented either through short descriptions or through short dramas, dramas of physical love, of maternal love, of sorrow, of jealousy. Like Kiki-la-Doucette and Toby-Chien, these animals, whatever they be and in whatever drama they are involved, always retain their own individuality, the particularities of their species and their fundamental likeness to all other living forms.

> *Human fantasy is limited; only reality ex-*
> *travagates without checks or bounds.*[24]

Colette's reactions to the plant world are similar to her reactions to the animal world. It is the life, not the death of the plant that interests her; it is the mystery of the plant world that intrigues her. Throughout her writings Colette speaks of flowers, but they receive special attention in *Flore et Pomone* (1943) and *Pour un Herbier* (1949). "The vegetable is not a mute kingdom," [25] writes Colette, and she describes with almost scientific precision the sound made by the falling petals of a rose, the sound made by the opening of irises. "The sound of an opening elytron, the sound of the delicate insect's leg, the sound of the dancing dead leaf, they were irises, in the filtered and propitious light, thousands of irises that were opening." [26]

Colette's knowledge of plants, of their names, their habits and the care needed to preserve them, is quite unusual. This knowledge comes from both observation and study. Sido's garden was Colette's first garden, but there were others. Whether in Franche-Comté or in Brittany, whether in Auteuil or in Provence, Colette had a garden which she tended herself. She also read and reread books on plants: *La Maison Rustique des Dames* by Madame Millet-Robinet, *L'Herbier de l'Amateur* by Lemaire, *Trochilides* by Lesson, *Histoire Naturelle—Les Plantes* by J. Constantin and F. Fardeau.

As in her animal tales, so in her portraits of flowers, Colette is rarely given to sentimentality. The individual flower is her starting point, and she obtains poetry from precision and analogy. Twenty-two different flowers are described by Colette in *Pour un Herbier*. Each is presented in a different way, depending on the associations Colette has with it. The lily, for example, recalls to Colette's mind a line of verse from Mallarmé's "L'Après-Midi d'un Faune": "Lilies! and one of you for artlessness." And so the portrait of the lily is mingled with Colette's reflections about Mallarmé. The rose evokes a whole series of associations: the flower of lovers; the difference between the florist's carefully trimmed rose and the natural rose; the exorbitant price of roses out of season; the names which Colette in secret gives to the rose: "Purple sin, small Apricot, Snow, Fairy, Black Beauty." [27]

In Colette's two-page description of an orchid [28] may be found the essence of that joy, sense of mystery and love which Colette felt for all living things. In *La Chatte*, the cat, Saha, was capable of seducing Alain, of having him prefer her to his wife. Not only can a cat seduce a man, in this world in which all living things are one, but it even happens that a flower can seduce a man. In "Orchidée," Colette relates the strange adventure of a jaguar hunter. One day the hunter was lying in wait for his prey. Bored with waiting, he raised his head and saw above him an orchid, a fantastic orchid. He put down his gun, climbed the difficult slope, and plucked the flower. As he came down and before he could reach for his gun, a royal jaguar advanced toward him, looked at him and continued on his way. Colette comments that she was told later that after his experience the jaguar hunter became a botanist. "I should have only liked to know whether he had converted out of gratitude toward

the clement jaguar, or whether the orchid, more power-
ful in charms than all other wild game, had forever
engulfed him in the regions where a man, between two
dangers, never fails to choose the worse." [29]

The seduction by a flower, like the seduction by a cat,
is a danger because it alienates man from the human
world, it brings him into contact with a primitive, elemental force. Once man has been thus seduced, once he
has felt the power and the beauty of this force, there is
no return.

As Colette proceeds with her description of the orchid,
the flower undergoes successive transformations. "It calls
to mind an octopus, a wooden shoe, a silver beard, an
owl, blood——" [30] The orchid that seduced the jaguar
hunter resembled "a bird, a crab, a butterfly, an evil
charm, a sexual organ, and perhaps even a flower." [31]
The orchid is a source of unlimited analogies. It is in
itself capable of suggesting the prodigious richness and
beauty of all living things, and Colette, as she contemplates the organization of the flower, is filled with the
sense of mystery. She asks herself the eternal questions:
"Someone—but who? . . . a hand, but which one?
Who? Where? Under what skies? Toward what end?
By what special permission does it practice its art of
mimesis?" [32]

The mystery remains. Colette can ask the questions,
but she cannot know, and perhaps she does not ever wish
to know, the answers. Here is mystery without mysti-
cism, mystery which is translated into literature through
precise descriptions and endless analogy, mystery which
is conveyed to the reader, as the familiar object becomes

suddenly extraordinary. This mystery was the source of Colette's joy and Colette's strength.

These flower portraits are in a sense the culmination of Colette's work. She never again achieved the same degree of descriptive perfection, the same depth of meaning. Yet, the flower portraits are too limited in scope, too specialized in their details, to warrant the title of "masterpieces." For masterpieces, it is necessary to turn to works which, though perhaps less perfect, are nevertheless in their very human content Colette's greatest legacy to literature.

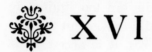 # XVI

The Masterpieces

> *. . . she, from whom I received the gift of*
> *shaking off the years as an apple tree its*
> *flowers.*[1]
>
> *Whence came her gift of definition, of pene-*
> *tration, and that form of authoritative ob-*
> *servation?* [2]

Next to the narrator, "Colette," Colette's greatest literary
creation is "Sido." And it is in those three works which
owe their existence both to "Sido" and to "Colette" that
the "Colette-Claudines" and the "Colette-Sidos," at last
stripped of their fictitious trimmings, emerge as both
real and mythical beings, embodying what is, at least in
the western world, the very essence of childhood and
motherhood. Although different in form and content,
La Maison de Claudine, Sido and *La Naissance du Jour*
are all suffused with the wisdom of "Sido," that wisdom
which could only attain effective literary transposition
when sufficient time had passed for Colette to begin,
undisturbed, her long dialogue with her mother.

Two of Colette's major themes, childhood and the conquest of self, reach their fullest expression in these works. With Sido as the starting point, Colette attempts to explore past, present and future. Her aim would seem to be twofold: to evoke the past through the perspective of the present in *La Maison de Claudine* and *Sido;* [3] and to foresee the future with the aid of the past in *La Naissance du Jour.* Also, however, one feels in these three works that Colette has a need for lucidity, a need to understand her mother, her past and herself, a need to commune with a presence and a world which had a certain "purity" and strength, "a world of which I have ceased to be worthy." [4]

The distance which separates *La Maison de Claudine* from the novels of the *Claudine* series is vast. There was, in 1922, no Monsieur Willy to obey, there was no longer any need for Colette deliberately to invent or to imagine. She had only to translate, in the light of a greater maturity and perspective, certain incidents of her childhood. So successful was her translation, that *La Maison de Claudine* is one of the books which best convey the poetry of childhood. *Maison,* as Colette uses the word in her title, refers specially to the house itself, the large house "topped by a lofty attic," in which the narrator and her family lived. *Maison* has a broader significance, as well. It is also the family of Claudine, the *pays natal* of Claudine, the childhood of Claudine. The first appearance of "Sido" in the opening chapter, following the description of the house and the silent, invisible presence of the children, establishes between "Sido" and the house both a real and a symbolic intimacy.

. . . this hand and this flame and the bowed, anxious head near the lamp, are the center and the secret womb from which radiates in decreasingly perceptible zones, in circles more and more remote from the essential light and vibration, the warm living room with its flora of cut branches, with its fauna of peaceful animals; the sonorous house, dry and crackling like newly baked bread; the garden, the village— Beyond, all is danger, all is solitude.[5]

"Sido" and the house, separately and together, are symbols of warmth, of security and of love.

The name "Claudine" recalls Colette's first novels, but there is little in common between the heroine of the *Claudine* series and the narrator of *La Maison de Claudine*. If Colette again uses the name "Claudine," it is both because she wants to give a new and truer image of her childhood and adolescence, wants the new "Claudine" to replace the old, and because the success of the "other" *Claudines* could be advantageous to the sale of the new book. In *La Maison de Claudine*, the name Claudine appears only in the title. The narrator refers to herself as "I," and she is, for her family, "the little one," "my treasure," or "*Minet-Chéri*." Colette referred to *La Maison de Claudine* as "my most veracious book; the one in which there is the least transposition." [6] It is undoubtedly true that the incidents related in this work are closer to the real incidents of Colette's youth than those related in *Claudine à l'Ecole*; but although the "I" of *La Maison de Claudine* is a more faithful portrait of Colette as a child than is the "other" Claudine, the "I" is nevertheless not entirely Colette as she was. The narrator of *La Maison de Claudine* is both the child and the woman, and because of this, there is a poetic stylization

both of incident and character which attests to the domi-
nating presence of the older, the writer Colette.

The definitive edition of *La Maison de Claudine*, published in 1930, contains thirty-five chapters ranging
from four to five pages in length, each a complete tale in
itself, each with its own title. The first twenty-six stories
contain anecdotes and descriptions relating to *La Maison
de Claudine*. The last nine are a mixture of animal tales
and short narratives centered on Colette's own daughter,
Bel-Gazou.[7]

There is no significant arrangement in the order of
the stories. The narrator is ten years old in one story and
fifteen in the next and then again ten or nine or eight.
Each story, each short drama, illustrates, illuminates
another aspect of her childhood, either her own private
world of odors, colors, words and games, or the world of
her family, of her village. These unrelated stories nevertheless form patterns: the repeated patterns of everyday
family life, familiar patterns which make the period of
childhood seem eternal. The narrator is the major link
between these stories. Much of the poetry of *La Maison
de Claudine* owes its origin to the narrator's double perspective: [8] sometimes completely involved in the past,
reliving the incident she is relating as if it were actually
occurring; sometimes stepping out of the story to comment on the past from the point of view of the present.
There is also a constant movement from the third person to the first, as the ubiquitous narrator becomes a
character in her story. Colette employs, in *La Maison de
Claudine*, the techniques of both her first-person and her
third-person writings.

More than in the other short stories, however, the den-

sity of Colette's prose, the extreme degree of condensation, make the small world of *La Maison de Claudine*
expandable, make it a symbol for the ideal world of
childhood. The mere mention of such words as "my
mother," "my province," "my house," evokes a series of
poetic images which carries the reader beyond *La Maison de Claudine* to his own real or imagined childhood.

This enlargement of the small world created within
the stories is also effected by the use Colette makes of
her concluding sentences or paragraphs. Sometimes, as
in "Jalousie," these final lines are a comment made by
the narrator on the preceding action, a comment made
from the perspective of the present. After a series of
particular incidents which show Le Capitaine's jealous
and impassioned love and Sido's reactions to her husband's outbursts, the narrator concludes, "But I still
laugh at their quarrels, because I am only fifteen, and
have not yet divined, beneath the eyebrow of the old
man, the ferocity of love, and on her fading cheeks, the
blushes of adolescence." [9] In this case, the method is
quite simple; Le Capitaine and Sido are brought from
their particular world into the world of all lovers.

Sometimes these concluding lines are lyrical, poetic
evocations of the past. In "Ma Mère et les Bêtes," for
example, Sido's passionate attachment to all living creatures is shown through a series of short anecdotes. And
the last paragraph, which begins, "The scene is still before my eyes, the garden with its warm walls, the last
black cherries hanging on the tree," [10] intensifies the
impression of the reality of what has gone before. Sometimes the narrator is not conspicuously present, and the
concluding lines pertain directly to the action of the

story. In "Ma Soeur aux Longs Cheveux," the narrator's sister, Juliette, is ill with a fever and when Sido approaches her bed, Juliette calls her Catulle Mendès. Sido is horrified by the fact that in delirium her daughter Juliette thinks only of strangers. The last line very simply ends the chapter: "And, as though overcome with shame, she [Sido] hid her face in her hands." [11] This ending gives the story a completeness and a tone of finality. It enlarges the scope of the incident by making it seem fictional rather than autobiographical.

Beyond this, and like all those works over which the figure of Sido presides, *La Maison de Claudine* provides, through concrete and poetized examples, a series of vivid images suggestive of a particular way of life, of an attitude toward life exemplified in the character of "Sido," who lived "swept by shadow and sunshine, bent by torments, resigned, unpredictable and generous, adorned with children, flowers and animals like a nutritious domain." [12] How close the "Sido" of Colette's writings is to the "real" woman, it is impossible to know. [13] Obviously words, gestures and attitudes have been stylized, accentuated and invented by Colette for the purpose of literature. In a manuscript of *Sido*, [14] the various changes made in certain of the lines spoken by "Sido" indicate that Colette is definitely not quoting her mother. However, it would seem that the generous and tolerant attitude toward life which characterizes the fictional "Sido" also characterized the original. Sido's humor, her courage, her constant concern for her children and husband, her scandalous sincerity and, above all, the constant joy she found in life, enabled her to create for herself and for her family that very simple yet magical world de-

scribed in *La Maison de Claudine*. This world no longer
has any real existence, the narrator says, and yet the
values implicit in it, the values which Sido created, exist
in memory and in the pages of Colette's book.

Although slightly different in form, *Sido* is, in theme
and atmosphere, very close to *La Maison de Claudine*.
In the three parts which compose this work—"Sido,"
"Le Capitaine" and "Les Sauvages"—the first-person
narrator attempts even more intensely than in *La Maison de Claudine* to understand her past, to understand
her parents and their relation to each other, to understand that heritage which they passed on to her and to
her brothers and sister.

The double time perspective still plays its part, although the use of the present tense, as the narrator
evokes her past, is even more frequent. Time is compressed and then expanded, as the narrator remembers
incidents, attitudes and words which seem to belong to
a five- or six-year period of her own childhood, with
leaps far back in time when she speaks of Sido's childhood.

Sido surrounded by her family, her animals and her
flowers, Sido speaking to the four winds, Sido, in reality
"small and round," assumes the stature of an immense
mother figure. It is much to Colette's credit that, despite
her many virtues, "Sido" is never presented as a saint.
Her humor and the narrator's humor save these stories
from any taint of sentimentality, from excessive adulation.

"Time is needed for the absent to take their true figure in our minds." [15] What the narrator discovers from this exploration of her past, from her renewed contact with it, is the true figure of her father and her resemblance to him. Like so many fathers in a household presided over by a strong, though in this case gentle, woman, Jules Colette was often in the background. In *La Maison de Claudine* and in the first part of *Sido*, he gives the impression of being a shadow, hovering near, but never quite coming onto, the stage. In Colette's evocations of her childhood and her family, as in her fictional world, it is the female element that predominates. Father and brothers, too, are relegated to inferior roles, they are part of the setting necessary for the main actors, who are Sido and her younger daughter.

Sido was her younger daughter's great love; Sido was her great teacher; her resemblance to Sido is one of acquired characteristics, achieved through deliberate emulation. "I imitated her manner. I still imitate it." [16] Her resemblance to Le Capitaine, to her little-known father, goes deeper; it is an inherited resemblance. "It seems strange to me, now, that I knew him so little. My attention, my fervor, directed toward Sido, only fitfully wandered from her. It was the same with my father." [17] Deeply, jealously in love with Sido, Le Capitaine subordinated all his life to this love. And although Sido returned his love, she never completely understood her husband—his superficial gaiety, his deep sadness—until after his death. "Poet and townsman," Le Capitaine was an exile in the concrete, natural world in which Sido and her younger children lived and revelled.

"Paternal lyricism, maternal humor and spontaneity, mingled and superimposed" [18]—Colette is proud of her inheritance. Yet, it is clear that the lyricism of her father, an apparently excessive, exaggerated use of words, which his daughter severely criticized, is almost completely absent in Colette's writings. Did she, as she indicates, overcome this tendency when Willy accused her of being "the last of the lyric poets?" [19] Or is it possible that Colette's double inheritance provided her with a natural equilibrium between Le Capitaine's verbal expansiveness and Sido's modesty and reticence?

"Les Sauvages," the last part of *Sido*, is a fitting conclusion to those works in which Colette speaks exclusively of her childhood. Her two elder brothers were *sauvages* in Rousseau's sense of the word, "frugal . . . sober and virtuous." The elder, Achille, never lost his taste for solitude, his tendency toward misanthropy. The younger, the "sylph," Léo, who showed early signs of a strong talent for music and daydreaming, was never able to live in a world which was not that of his childhood. At the age of sixty-three, he was still a "sylph," a *sauvage*, for whom the only reality that had meaning was the *maison de Claudine*, the house at Saint-Sauveur-en-Puisaye. Léo, like Colette, was constantly searching for this lost paradise. But unlike her brother, who, when he returned to his birthplace, discovered with horror that the gate no longer squeaked because it had been oiled, Colette was able to hear within her the inimitable voice of her mother, a voice which grew even more distinct with Sido's death, and this voice was one of the keys that unlocked the door of the *maison de Claudine*.

*She is in full possession of that world which
we have all, at one time, merited, created
and lost.*[20]

A year after the death of Sido, Colette became a mother.
Although most of the stories that deal with her daughter, Bel-Gazou, were written before *La Maison de Claudine*, they form a logical sequel to it, presenting, as they
do, the handing down of Sido's wisdom to a second generation.

The relation between Bel-Gazou, Sido and Colette is
both close and complex. There is an obvious association
in Colette's mind between herself as a mother and Sido,
between herself as a child and Bel-Gazou. Bel-Gazou is
one of the strongest links in the chain that binds Colette
to Sido and to her own childhood.

The form of the Bel-Gazou stories, an anecdote or a
series of anecdotes followed by a general conclusion, is
similar to the form of the stories in *La Maison de Claudine*.

There are many differences between Colette's childhood and that of her daughter. Bel-Gazou was born in
Paris twelve months before the first World War; Bel-
Gazou is an only child; Bel-Gazou has a winter home
and a summer home; Bel-Gazou has an English nurse.
These differences affect the setting of the anecdotes, but
they do not affect Colette's double theme, which is essentially the same in these stories as in *La Maison de
Claudine:* the privileged world of childhood and the delicate relation between mother and daughter.

Colette shares with Sido the rare blend of love and

respect for her offspring. However, because the pleasure Colette takes in her daughter is both "maternal and literary," [21] she is perhaps less spontaneous, more calculating, in her reactions and her words than was her own mother.

"Maternal" or "literary," Colette's concern is the same. The more Bel-Gazou reveals the intense sensuous and poetic life of the child, the happier are Colette the mother and Colette the writer. "I see, I see the song!" cries Bel-Gazou, holding to her ear a hollow nut tossed up by the waves. "It is thin as a hair, it is thin as a blade of grass." [22] In Bel-Gazou's rapture and Bel-Gazou's pleasure reside Colette's maternal joy and anxiety, Colette's own literary and personal challenge.

> Next year Bel Gazou will be over nine years old. She will have ceased to proclaim those inspired truths that baffle her educators. Each day carries her further away from her first full, wise and mistrustful life which loftily disdains experience, good counsel and ordinary wisdom. Next year she will return to the sands that gild her, to the salt butter and the foaming cider. She will again find her dilapidated hut, and her city feet will again put on their naturally corned soles, slowly toughened on the flint and on the clipped grasses. But she may perhaps not find her childish subtlety and the superiority of her senses that know how to taste a perfume, touch a color and see "thin as a hair, thin as a blade of grass" the cadence of an imaginary song. [23]

When Bel-Gazou loses "her childish subtlety and the superiority of her senses," when she loses "that world which we have all, at one time, merited, created and lost," then will her mother tremble. With the child Bel-Gazou, as with the animals, Colette is at ease; but what will her reactions be to an adolescent Bel-Gazou, already exiled from the world of childhood? And what will Bel-Gazou herself become when she has lost contact with this world? These, it would seem, are Colette's maternal preoccupations as she comments on her daughter's future. There is something more. Bel-Gazou, the child, assists Colette in her exploration of her own childhood, provides her with sudden associations and intuitions. Colette uses Bel-Gazou as a means of communication with the past. The inevitable loss of childhood is more appalling to the writer than to the mother. This need not necessarily be taken as evidence of an interested love. Colette "uses" Sido in much the same way, with, however, this very important distinction, that Bel-Gazou is alive and Sido dead. Both in life and in art, Colette, it would seem, found it easier and more profitable to be a daughter than a mother.

In *La Naissance du Jour*,[24] Colette attempts, with Sido's aid, to create her own values for herself. *La Naissance du Jour* is the account of a woman who, having arrived at a certain age, is forced to set new limits to her world. It is a spiritual odyssey, the story of the creation of a way of life by a woman who is forced to abdicate and who, guided by the examples found in her mother's letters, discovers that even in abdication there is joy. From the beginning of *La Naissance du Jour*, Sido is taken as a model of "purity," as a storehouse of that wisdom for which the narrator, in her long monologue, is searching.

If one may accept Colette's word,[25] the letters presented in *La Naissance du Jour* were written by the real

Sido to her daughter. *Le Figaro Littéraire*, in its special "Hommage à Colette," January 24, 1953, contains a group of letters also written by Sido to Colette.[26] One of these, dated August 21, 1907, appears in *La Naissance du Jour*, but with considerable changes and polishings. It may be assumed, then, that Colette rewrote, for *La Naissance du Jour*, all the letters which she quotes; in any case, the "real" letters in *Le Figaro Littéraire* reveal a remarkable similarity in feeling and expression between Sido and her daughter. Both women have an unusual gift of observation and a very keen sensitivity to flowers, animals and weather. There is also, in Sido's letters, that mixture of tenderness and reticence which characterizes most of Colette's writings. Certain passages indicate that Sido had a talent for writing and an originality which perhaps her daughter both emulated and inherited.[27] Sentences such as "Cats are divine beasts and consequently misunderstood," [28] or "I also used to say to you that when you entered a room in which I was, it became brighter," [29] might well have been written by Colette.

La Naissance du Jour is a hymn to life, presented as a slow, poetical self-analysis. "No fear, not even the fear of ridicule, stops me from writing these lines which will be (I am willing to run the risk) published. Why stop the hand that has gathered, for so many years, what I know about myself and what I try to hide, what I invent and what I divine?" [30] In this book, Colette creates a very complex first-person narrator. The complexity is all the greater because the narrator bears the name "Colette," she is no longer wearing an obvious mask. "Now, legally, literally, and familiarly, I have no more than one name which is my own." [31] She is, however, wearing the mask of "Colette."

When *La Naissance du Jour* was published, the critics, heedless of the warning, "Do you imagine, in reading my books, that I am drawing my portrait? Patience; it is only my model," [32] considered the work completely autobiographical. Subsequent publications, and particularly Maurice Goudeket's *Près de Colette*, have shown that *La Naissance du Jour* is far from being pure autobiography. Throughout the book runs the refrain "Is this then the end of my militant life?" [33] the "militant life" which the narrator is renouncing is love. However, Colette spent the summer during which she wrote this with Maurice Goudeket in Provence, and there was, for her, no question of the renunciation of love. In this work, then, Colette is not describing a present state, she is projecting a future one, she is attempting, in advance, to come to terms with herself, with love and with life, she is reconciling herself to the inevitable. [34]

Unfortunately, because Colette had promised her publishers a novel, and did not want to disappoint them completely, *La Naissance du Jour* includes a fragmentary love story involving three people: the story of the relationship between Vial and the narrator, between Hélène and the narrator, between Vial and Hélène. Vial loves the narrator, Hélène loves Vial, and the narrator attempts to bring Vial and Hélène together. In the background appear contemporary artists and their mistresses, who come to call on the narrator, eat with the narrator, swim with the narrator. This secondary drama, these minor characters and incidents, add nothing to *La Naissance du Jour*. They give the work an organization, a slender plot, which only interferes with the deeper rhythm of the passing days and nights.

Vial, however, plays a special role in *La Naissance du Jour*. Colette dramatizes the narrator's renunciation of love in a dialogue with Vial, a dialogue which begins in the evening and ends with the birth of a new day. In refusing Vial, the narrator has refused all men, she has definitely rejected the world of physical love.

Into the almost uninterrupted monologue, Colette has succeeded in interweaving all her themes: Sido, childhood, animals, death, the beauty of nature and love. Her prose is here at its best. As in *Les Vrilles de la Vigne*, Colette is very little hampered by the restriction of a conventional plot. Her struggles with the craft of fiction, with the need of controlling her natural lyricism, have had their effects, and her new lyricism, because it is more restrained, has an even greater force and can convey deeper meanings. "For to dream, and then to enter into reality, is only to change the position and the seriousness of a scruple." [35] With her habitual discretion, her uncanny sense of the proper distance between emotion and expression, Colette discusses her own commonplace, eternal themes.

Each one of Sido's letters exemplifies an attitude toward life, contains a moral lesson, which stimulates the narrator's monologue. The latter has reached "a peaceful plateau" in her life; she has attained the age when "a woman can only be enriched." [36] For the first time since she was sixteen years old, she must live and die "without my life or my death depending on love." [37] What is to fill this gap? How is she to live? To these questions, Sido's letters provide answers. Sido, filled with awe and sadness in the presence of a beautiful child, commented in a letter, "Great lovers, confronted with the object of their passion, behave in the same way. Am I then, in my fashion, a great lover?" [38] Sido wrote to her daughter, "Love is not an honorable feeling," [39] Sido, who knew, who understood, the ultimate lesson, "We possess by abstaining and only by abstaining." [40]

It is against the background of these letters that the narrator confronts the young people who swarm around her, that she confronts her solitude, that she writes and lives through "a beautiful season of the year, but above all a beautiful season of my life." [41] Death, suffering and illness are all foreseen, and are dismissed as uninteresting. "Death does not interest me—not even my own." [42] Only life is interesting, only "the birth of a new day" is worthy of complete attention.

At the end of the monologue, the narrator is on the threshold of a new life. She has witnessed the birth of a new day in the splendor of Provence, she has witnessed her own slow rebirth, and she has learned that to renounce is to lose, but that to lose is to gain and indeed that there is real gain only through loss. The experience of privation is a new experience, thus an acquisition, a positive value. The conquest of self is the greatest victory, the greatest joy a human being can know. She has put the problems clearly, she has lived through her all-night talk with Vial; she has come out of her experience having attained a new equilibrium. With Sido's aid, she has found within herself sufficient strength for the healing of her wound. She is prepared to accept the inevitable, but she is also prepared to find, in solitude and old age, new joys. *La Naissance du Jour* is the account of a victory. Is Colette, at last, worthy of Sido?

Never again did Colette achieve that perfect balance of form and content, that delicate relation between fact and fiction, between poetry and prose, which make of *La Maison de Claudine, Sido* and *La Naissance du Jour* her indisputable masterpieces. No discussion of Colette's writings, however, no list of her masterpieces, can be complete without some mention of her most original contribution to the subject of sensuality, *Le Pur et l'Impur*.[43] It is, in many ways, a curious book and, as Colette's only "treatise," something of a phenomenon when compared to the rest of her works.

Nothing, at first glance, could seem further removed either from the childhood world of *La Maison de Claudine* and *Sido*, or from the stoical, heroic atmosphere of *La Naissance du Jour* than the opium smokers, homosexuals and Don Juans of *Le Pur et l'Impur*. Yet, with a minimal use of paradox, it can be shown that *Le Pur et l'Impur* belongs, in spirit and point of view, with the Sido-dominated books, that it is, in fact, an extreme and illuminating variation on the theme of love and purity.

Le Pur et l'Impur is neither an apology for nor an explanation of the various forms of love that Colette explores. Using her favorite medium, anecdotes, Colette presents, through actual dialogue or through reported or remembered incidents, examples of so-called "impure" relationships. Colette's tone is so undramatic, her attitude toward the subject apparently so free of emotional involvement, that what sometimes appears as gratuitous self-indulgence in the works of Proust, Gide and particularly Jean Genêt, is totally absent from *Le Pur et l'Impur*. Colette might be discussing a weird hat or an abnormal vegetable, although there is no evidence of any intention on her part to poke fun at her subject.

One of the primary reasons for Colette's originality is that she seems to have no a priori moral-medical-psychological reactions to or convictions about opium smokers and homosexuals, and that she does not take her subject as dead seriously as modern psychologists and sociologists would undoubtedly demand. The only principle in which she firmly believes is that there is only one animal, one love and one vice.

Colette describes with equal sympathy Madame Charlotte, the woman who feigns pleasure in order to please her young lover; Damien, the prototype of Colette's unwritten play on Don Juan as misogynist; La Chevalière; Renée Vivien; the ladies of Llangollen. She presents impartially the women who love women, the old and young women whose affections are exclusively masculine, jealousy, her own and others'. She adventures through the domain of the sensual and the sexual, attempting to show the relation between love and pleasure, between joy and sadness, between purity and impurity.

"The word 'pure' has not disclosed to me its intelligible meaning," [44] is Colette's very honest conclusion. The word is repeated over and over again in *Le Pur et l'Impur* and in *La Naissance du Jour*, and the various ways in which it is used are revealing. Colette speaks of the "purity of those who give lavishly of themselves," [45] the "purity of those who have not committed infractions"; [46] of Sido, she says, "I am her impure survivor." [47] Sido's prodigality, Sido's patience are attributes of her "purity," a purity which Colette feels is lacking in herself in the same way that she feels "unworthy" of the world of *La Maison de Claudine*.

There is, then, something more than time that separates Colette from the lost paradise of childhood, from a true resemblance to her mother. Is it very simply that Colette is condemning her multiple liaisons, her three marriages? Why do the characters in *Le Pur et l'Impur*, lovers all, use this word so freely? "Our infinity was so pure that I never thought of death." [48] "Envelope me; as soon as I have nothing more to hide from you, I feel pure." [49] Why does Colette herself use the word when she comments on the ladies of Llangollen and their initial "turbulent and pure passion," [50] and on Pepe who, watching the young men emerge from the subway, "tasted a purer pleasure than the amateurs of young factory girls on the rue de la Paix, because he neither moved nor spoke"? [51] She says of the English reading public's reaction to the ladies of Llangollen, "Jealous of such an imperturbable tenderness, they insist that the two faithful lovers lack purity, but what do they mean by purity?" [52] Of the group of male homosexuals which she frequents, she muses, "When I was alone with my 'monsters' I called 'pure' and loved the atmosphere that banished women. But, in this manner, I would have also loved the purity of the desert and the prison. The prison and the desert are not within everyone's range." [53]

Why are Sido, the ladies of Llangollen, Pepe and the "monsters" pure, and not Colette? Why was Chéri pure? What is there in common between the purity of Sido and the purity of the "monsters"?

In all these contexts, the word "pure" or "purity" carries with it a sense of exclusiveness. It seems to refer to a privileged domain or state, reserved only for a few, free from anything extraneous to the ruling passion. It would appear that, for Colette, the world of the ladies of Llangollen and of her "monsters" is the closest approximation she has found in adult life to the world of Sido and childhood. Purity, thus, does have a moral connotation, although it is not the conventional one. The protagonists of the anecdotes in *Le Pur et l'Impur* are pure in the same way that Sido is pure, that Chéri is pure; they live in an independent world to which they give themselves completely. Never is Sido's attention distracted from the daily adventures of her house, her garden and her village; never is Chéri distracted from the thought of Léa; never are the ladies of Llangollen and the "monsters" distracted from the presence of the loved one.

Was Colette's mobility a lack of fidelity? Did the very fact of being a writer, of constantly masking and disguising herself, deprive her of the right to enter, as Colette, into the kingdom of the pure?

This feeling of not being pure may well have been one of Colette's personal concerns. Quite often the reader may sense it in her novels, short stories, anecdotes, meditations and reminiscences. It is not merely by chance, however, that the works in which it stands out most clearly should also be Colette's masterpieces. Paradoxically, by their very existence, they attest to her long and patient efforts to eliminate all impurities from her work, to discover, behind all the masks, her own voice and her own world. Despite her self-doubt, Colette, by virtue of her fidelity to her work, was indeed one of the pure.

 **XVII**

Sorcery and Sagacity

> *The important thing for me is to lay bare
> and bring to light what no human eye be-
> fore mine has looked upon.*[1]
>
> *. . . we will never look enough, never
> accurately enough, never passionately
> enough.*[2]

"Classical,"[3] "spontaneous,"[4] "natural,"[5] "ornate,"[6] "nonexistent"[7]—Colette's style has been described in numerous contradictory ways. And the critics are not lacking in great names when they wish to find comparisons: the Latin authors, Martial, Horace; the French authors, Bossuet, La Fontaine, Pascal, Racine, Rousseau, Chateaubriand, Rimbaud. By selecting sentences from the mass of Colette's writings, one would indeed be able to compare her to many of the great French writers of the seventeenth, eighteenth and nineteenth centuries. This in itself would not constitute a proof of Colette's own greatness, and still less would it help in an attempted definition of her style.[8]

Throughout Colette's work runs the complaint of the writer for whom writing, although a financial and eventually a psychological necessity, was always an arduous, often a painful task. According to Monsieur Goudeket, during the years which he spent with Colette (1928–1954), she worked most often in the afternoon, from three o'clock to six o'clock. And Colette relates in *L'Etoile Vesper* that her *anciens livres* were written between ten in the evening and three in the morning. Three to five hours of writing per day is not a great deal of time if one considers the extensiveness of the *Oeuvres complètes* of Colette, her extra-literary activities and her correspondence. It would seem, therefore, as if Colette had, to some extent, exaggerated the difficulty, though not the intensity and the care, with which she wrote.

An examination of a manuscript of *Sido* [9] and a comparison between this manuscript and the definitive edition of *Sido* show that Colette's rewriting always entailed elimination and condensation. What Colette concentrated on, in a long sentence, was perfecting the sequence and the tense of verbs, and, in general, finding the appropriate word. She never changed the basic image; again according to Monsieur Goudeket, at Colette's first writing the same image was already present as in the final version.

In the manuscript of *Sido*, the first words of a sentence in which the narrator speaks of two hidden springs which she reveres, "Je voudrais qu'une gorgée imaginaire de leur eau . . ." ("I wish that an imagined draft of their water . . ."), are crossed out and changed to "Rien qu'à parler d'elles, je souhaite qu'une gorgée imaginaire de leur eau . . ." ("The very mention of them makes me hope that an imagined draft of their water . . ."). The original image remains. The change is one in subtlety. With the substitution of "Rien qu'à parler d'elles" for "Je voudrais," the sentence takes on a temporal third dimension; to the past and the future is added the present. "Rien qu'à parler d'elles, je souhaite qu'une gorgée imaginaire de leur eau, froide à trois heures du matin, noire sous l'herbe, m'emplisse la bouche au moment de tout finir et que j'emporte, avec moi, cette gorgée imaginaire." ("The very mention of them makes me hope that an imagined draft of their water, cold, at three in the morning, black under the grass, may fill my mouth at the moment of death and that I may carry with me that imagined draft.") The definitive version reads, "Rien qu'à parler d'elles, je souhaite que leur saveur m'emplisse la bouche au moment de tout finir, et que j'emporte, avec moi, cette gorgée imaginaire" [10] ("The very mention of them makes me hope that their savor may fill my mouth . . ."). Between the manuscript and the final version, Colette has eliminated about twelve words and the repetition of "gorgée imaginaire."

Such examples of rather extensive rewriting and reworking are not too frequent in this particular manuscript. One would, of course, have to see the different drafts that preceded and followed the manuscript, and which no longer exist, in order to arrive at any definite conclusions as to how Colette really composed.

Colette has often been accused of a certain pedantry in her animal and vegetal vocabulary. Her knowledge of plant and animal names was vast, and she conscientiously uses the exact, the erudite word whenever it is needed, *i.e.*, *aiguail* (dewdrop), *anatife* (barnacle, on ships), *bondrée* (a pern or honey-buzzard), *pélargonium* (the plant, pelargonium), *pholade* (the bivalve mollusk, pholas piddock). Colette's ultimate goal was always that the word cling as closely as possible to the thing described, or to the emotion felt. "Signs wandering in the air, sometimes the words, summoned, deign to descend, flock together, settle—thus the little miracle that I call the golden egg, the bubble, the flower, seems to form: a sentence worthy of what it wanted to describe." [11] The bird, the flower, the animal that Colette is reconstructing through words is more important to her than the words themselves. Art, Colette declares, did not rule her life. "Aside from the art that may be concealed in the painted color, a beloved text, a sound, a form, art has had very little influence on my life." [12] If her own art is so carefully worked out and so precise, it is because of her infinite respect and love for the living thing.

There is a very definite moral-aesthetic relationship which explains the artisan-like way in which Colette worked. In the beginning of *La Naissance du Jour*, the reader is told how the aging Sido refused to visit her beloved daughter, because her rose cactus, which bloomed only once every four years, was about to come into flower. In *L'Etoile Vesper*, Colette tells of a conversation that took place in the garden of the Palais Royal, on the day of the German occupation of Paris, between "the man with the cages" and a civilian. The civilian, a stranger to the Palais Royal, was shocked to discover that "the man with the cages" seemed completely unaware of the Germans. "Mon-

sieur," the latter replied to the stranger's remon-
strances, "my major concern, today as other days, is the
care of my canaries. Just think, my canaries are Saxon,
Monsieur, Saxon." [13] Sido's total preoccupation with the
rose cactus, the total preoccupation of "the man with
the cages" with his canaries, their refusal to divert their
loving attention from the cherished object to the seemingly more important event, symbolize the relationship
between Colette and the world. Colette has been accused
of not dealing, in her works, with the important political
and human problems of her time, and of concentrating
too much on her own small and particular domain of
love and lovers, of nature and its manifestations. And to
this accusation is always appended the reproach that
Colette is indifferent to questions of morality, that she
is incapable, perhaps, of dealing with them. But in her
aimless "promenade," and "meditations," her constant
evocation of the past, are the evidences of Colette's long
dialogue with the real, with those things—love, a flower,
an animal—which held her attention as intensely as her
mother's was held by the rose cactus. Nothing is more
"real" or more important to Colette than this contemplation of the actual, than this relationship which the
human being establishes, in solitude, with the world of
living things. The implicit moral imperative is, again,
"*Regarde*," and the accompanying aesthetic imperative
and the key to her style is also "*Regarde*"; "Look"—and,
prepared to struggle with words, faithfully reproduce
the object, the sensation.

This moral and aesthetic imperative, this insistence
on precision accounts, in great part, for the poetic quality that permeates Colette's evocations of childhood. If

Colette wishes to re-enter the domain of her childhood, it is not only because she wants to recall or remember the past, but also because she wishes to feel, to "regard" the past with the feelings and the eyes of the child. "Children and the insane have an incontestable superiority over us. They stand in immediate relation to color, to sensation, to events. We re-create the world. They present a universe directly felt and perceived." [14] This immediate "relation" with the real which, as has been seen in *La Maison de Claudine* and in the Bel-Gazou stories, is the prerogative of childhood, becomes for Colette the goal of the artist. "For what are we, we so-called artists, if not adults who remember their own childhood souls?" [15] Therein lies Colette's originality in an epoch which proclaims that the essential function of the artist is to "re-create" reality.

The style, then, is directed by this intention. The resuscitation of childhood through sensations, usually familiar odors, necessarily demands the use of the concrete. Once the concrete object has aroused the sensation, the sensation opens the world of childhood and one may enter the realm of the poetry of memory.

> Porte plutôt à tes narines le parfum invariable de ces violettes changeantes et regarde, en respirant le philtre qui abolit les années, regarde comme moi ressusciter et grandir devant toi les printemps de ton enfance. . . . Je revois des prés, des bois profonds que la première poussée des bourgeons embrume d'un vert insaisissable, des ruisseaux froids, des sources perdues, bues par le sable aussitôt que nées, des primevères de Pâques, des jeannettes jaunes au coeur safrané, et des violettes, des violettes, des violettes. . . Je revois une enfant silencieuse que le printemps enchantait déjà d'un bonheur sauvage, d'une triste et mystérieuse

joie. . . Une enfant prisonnière, le jour, dans une école, et qui échangeait des jouets, des images, contre les premiers bouquets de violettes des bois, noués d'un fil de coton rouge, apportés par les petites bergères des fermes environnantes . . . Violettes à courte tige, violettes blanches et violettes bleues et violettes d'un blanc-bleu veiné de nacre mauve, violette de coucou anémiques et larges, qui haussent sur de longues tiges leurs pâles corolles inodores. . . Violettes de février, fleuries sous la neige, déchiquetées, roussies de gel, laideronnes, pauvresses parfumées. . . O violettes de mon enfance! [16]

Or rather carry to your nostrils the invariable perfume of these changing violets and look, while breathing the philter that abolishes the years, look as I do at the spring-times of your childhood which resuscitate and grow before you. . . I see again meadows, deep woods, that the thrusting of the buds covers with a subtle green, cold streams, hidden springs drunk by the sand as soon as they are born, Easter primroses, yellow spinning-jennies with a saffron heart and violets, violets, violets— I see again a silent child whom springtime already enchanted with a wild happiness, a sad and mysterious joy— A child held prisoner during the day in a school and who exchanged games and pictures for the first bouquets of wood violets, tied with a thread of red cotton, brought by the young shepherdesses of the neighboring farms— Short-stemmed violets, white violets, purple violets, whitish-blue violets veined with mauve mother-of-pear, anemic and large violets of the barren strawberry plant which raise their pale, odorless petals on their long stems— Violets of February in bloom under the snow, mangled, reddened by the frost, ugly, poor and fragrant violets— O violets of my childhood!

So as not to break the momentum of the passage, Co-lette uses three dots rather than periods. The rhythm of Colette's prose invariably has its source in the repetition

of words, or word groups: "Look—look—I see again—I
see again—a child—a child—violets—violets—violets,
violets, violets—O violets." "The philter which abolishes the years" allows Colette to move from odor to
vision, from the perfume of violets to springtime, from
springtime to the child and back again to violets, violets
of all kinds, violets of all colors, through the constant
repetition of the word "violets" itself. The word, as in
an incantation, acquires magical powers. It is capable of
conjuring up the real. At the same time, the repetition
translates the child's reactions to the multitude and the
variety of the violets. "The wild happiness," the "sad
and mysterious joy" of the "silent child," of the "im-
prisoned child," set the inner emotional tone of the passage. Not until Colette has reseen the child, not until she
has recaptured the soul of the child, do the violets assume their reality, do they become particular, individual, that is to say, real violets.

By the accumulation of very precise images, Colette
appears to move from the domain of the real to the
domain of the fantastic. She takes one to the point where
so much realism becomes, by its abundance, surrealism
and poetry. It is inevitable that when Colette evokes her
childhood, her sentences become longer, more involved,
as she attempts, recapturing the past through a sensation of the present, to unite the child's ability to feel
with the writer's ability to express.

Published in 1908, the above passage is typical of Colette's early lyrical style. Twenty years later, in *La
Naissance du Jour*, there appear the same procedures,
the same accumulation of images, the same repetitions.
Colette's syntax has, however, with the passage of time,

become more complicated, her images more condensed and the experience or sensation she is describing more intense.

The sixth chapter of *La Naissance du Jour* opens with a letter from Sido to her daughter in which Sido describes the burning of a neighbor's barn. As there is nothing that she can do to help, she takes her morning coffee and contemplates the beautiful conflagration—for Sido loves cataclysms. This letter is followed by four pages of dialogue between the narrator, "Colette," and the young artist, Hélène Clément. Hélène, in love with Vial, wants to be confirmed in her opinion that if Vial is incapable of loving her, it it because he is in love with Madame Colette. Hélène is on the verge of tears.

> Elle me suppliait de comprendre, de ne point l'obliger à parler; mais je cessai soudain de m'occuper d'elle en tant qu'Hélène Clément. Je lui rendis sa place dans l'univers, parmi les spectacles d'autrefois dont j'avais été le spectateur anonyme ou l'orgueilleux responsable. Cette honnête forcenée ignorera toujours qu'elle fut digne d'affronter dans ma mémoire les larmes de délice d'un adolescent,—le premier choc du feu sombre, à l'aurore, sur une cime de fer bleu et de neige violette,—le desserrement floral d'une main plissée de nouveau-né,—l'écho d'une note unique et longue, envolée d'un gosier d'oiseau, basse, d'abord, puis si haute que je la confondais, dans le moment où elle se rompit, avec le glissement d'une étoile filante,—et ces flammes, ma très chère, ces pivoines échevelées de flammes que l'incendie secouait sur ton jardin. . . Tu t'attablais contente, cuiller en main, "puisqu'il ne s'agissait que de paille." [17]

She begged me to understand, and not to oblige her to speak; but I suddenly ceased to be interested in her as Hélène Clément. I gave her back her place in the universe, among the bygone spectacles of which I was the anony-

mous spectator or the proud originator. This honest mad-
woman will never know that she was worthy of confront-
ing, in my memory, the adolescent's tears of pleasure—the
first shock of the somber fire, at dawn, on a peak of iron
blue and violet snow—the floral opening of a new-born
baby's puckered hand—the echo of a long, single note
which took wing from a bird's throat, at first low, then so
high that I confused it, in the moment when it broke off,
with the gliding of a falling star—and those flames, my
dearly beloved, those extravagant, peony-like flames, that
the fire shook off on your garden— You were sitting down
at your table, content, a spoon in your hand, "because it
was only straw."

In these sixteen lines, Colette has brought together her
relationship with Hélène Clément, her indifference to
the present, her preoccupation with the past and Sido's
letter on the burning of a barn. The rapid succession of
condensed and seemingly unrelated images forces the
reader's attention. Hélène Clément has become for Colette a spectacle among others; Hélène's attitude does
not evoke from the narrator either pity or compassion,
but a disciplined stream of associated memories. These
imaged memories are all related to each other and, of
course, to Hélène Clément. Hélène, about to break into
wild sobs, is associated by Colette with various acts of
opening, of outpouring and of falling: the tears, the first
shock, the floral opening of a hand, the echo which
breaks like a falling star, and the "extravagant, peony-
like flames" which descend on the garden. The relationship between these images is based on a movement
which is essentially the same for all. The magic of Colette's style is real magic, precisely because she never
leaves the domain of the real. These associated memory

images all contain a source of joy or beauty, and it is evident that, here at least, what interests Colette is not Hélène's quite genuine sorrow, but her vision of Hélène as form and movement. "Have you inherited my love of cataclysms?" [18] writes Sido in her letter, and this is Colette's answer. What this example of Colette's more evolved and complicated style reveals is that for Colette, as for Sido, the contemplation of the world is devoid of sentimentality. It is a detached contemplation, in which the beauty of the spectacle—whether of flames or of tears about to flow—is all-important. Colette's lyricism is not a lyricism of the heart, but rather of the eye. It is a song sung in praise of the thing in itself, of inherent beauty.

Both in the first-person writings, in which Colette, by means of lengthy, cadenced sentences, pursues her endless promenade through memory, and in the third-person writings, in which, through condensed narrative and rapid dialogue, she presents the duels of her animal-like lovers, it is the particular use of the suggestively familiar, of the real, that characterizes Colette's style. Colette always remains within the realm of the banal, the ordinary, but so well does she describe the banal, that it becomes the unusual, it takes on the poetic quality with which we tend to endow the unknown. Colette's poetry is the poetry of the everyday object, the common experience, just as her wisdom, which she transmits through her many aphorisms, is a practical wisdom derived from these objects and experiences.

Style, Marcel Proust has said, is a quality of vision, the revelation of a particular universe. Any analysis of

Colette's style reveals that her particular quality of vision emanates from the distance, the reserve, the modesty, which Colette maintains between the words and herself. This distance translates, in aesthetic terms, Colette's personal relation to reality, her respect for life.

In the words of Andre Gide, "She never mistakes for inspiration that rather facile effusion, that poetic rapture, with which most women authors are content, and which results in our being severe with them because they feel nothing but complacency and acquiescence toward their own work." [19]

It is Colette's aim to bring to the reader's attention that which the human eye has not before looked upon or rather that which, although constantly seen, is never really observed, and because Colette both cherishes and respects the real, she treats it with loving care, she preserves its reality and, in so doing, creates her own magical art.

To speak of the "world" of Balzac or the "world" of Proust is to speak of the totality of their work, of the adventure of their characters in time and space, of their particular vision and its ordering within a coherent whole. One cannot speak in the same way of the world of Colette. Balzac and Proust, are, in a certain sense of the word, visionaries. They use the "real" world as a point of departure for their own created world, as a stepping-stone to something else. Colette, on the contrary, never leaves the "real." Indeed, her entire effort would seem to be directed toward an always closer contact with it. Her attention is always focused on the concrete, on that which can be seen, touched, smelled, tasted. Both Colette's art and the equilibrium and wisdom which she finally attains are dependent on her particular point of view.

> These innovators are much too busy with their completely pneumatic function which consists in expelling all the air from their pictures and forgetting that mysterious, slightly divine thing, called perspective, that miracle which suddenly, four centuries ago, detached the painted figure from the wall to which it was flatly affixed, filled with a necessary breath the portraits of trees and of mountains and pushed back to the edge of the sky the cloud, the undulating plain or the waves of the sea.[20]

In this paragraph, Colette is criticizing the flatness of cubist painting. The importance she accords to the notion of perspective may guide evaluation of what Colette succeeded in doing in her own work. The cubists rearrange reality, they create new intellectual perspectives by eliminating natural perspectives and thereby change the habitual relationships of things. Colette's use of perspective is much simpler, but none the less original. Usually, in literature as in art, perspectives are deformed, are deliberately deformed so as to express the author's view of reality. Colette has no particular view of reality, hence her originality. The reader has nothing to interpret or to reconstruct in Colette's descriptions of the outer world. He has only to marvel at the fact that she has seen so much. Colette's perspective comes from the direct, immediate relation between the eye and the thing, the eye and the word. Her realism, therefore, is perhaps the truest form of realism in French literature. She does not set out to portray a particular class of society or a particular kind of individual, nor does she intend to select certain significant details for her descriptions. Painstakingly she describes the entire object, the complete sensation. If Colette's characters belong to a certain section of society, it is because Colette knows that section of society, and feels competent to render fully only the reality of those people about whom she knows a great deal. They have, however, no greater claim to her attention than those animals, plants or objects that she knows just as well. The abundance of Colette's work stems in part from the fact that there exists for her no hierarchy in subject matter. The perspective never changes. It is always a question of reconstructing with words the real object, the real event, the real emotion. Colette can never quench her "thirst for the prodigious real." [21]

In a preface to Renée Hamon's book, *Aux Iles de la Lumière*, Colette answers Mademoiselle Hamon's honest admission, "But I don't know what one should put in a book." Her answer, although it applies specifically to the task of the reporter, is significant.

> Neither do I. I have acquired a very few notions only on what it is better not to put in. Paint only what you have seen. Look for a long time at those things that give you pleasure, still longer at those that give you pain. Try to be faithful to your first impression. Don't make a fetish of the "rare word." Don't tire yourself by lying. The lie develops the imagination and imagination is the death of the reporter. Take notes— No, don't take notes. Beware of "embellishments," beware of indiscreet poetry. Don't write your articles over there, they will be unrecognizable when you return here. One does not write a love story while one is making love—— [22]

Colette herself always tried to follow this very simple, almost completely negative credo, although there are in her writings occasional "rare words," occasional "embellishments." The adolescents, the women, the men, the animals, the flowers that compose her cast are never completely invented. They reflect the tendencies and attitudes of Colette herself or they are the composite images of the real people, the real animals, the real flowers that she observed. It is not surprising that the most successful of Colette's literary creations are "Sido" and the narrator, "Colette," for they were the best known, the most easily observable, both with the outer and the inner eye, of her models. Colette's mistrust of imagination was both her greatest weakness and her greatest strength.

Just as Colette's characters are always rooted in the real world, so the settings of her works, from Montigny to the Palais Royal are, under real or assumed names, always places which she knew well. Whether it be the countryside of Brittany or Provence, or the closed, garish rooms and apartments of the Parisian demimonde at the turn of the century, or Colette's own apartment in the Palais Royal, the setting is always precisely described and carefully dated.

Only the world of childhood escapes from time, is somehow out of time. And this is because the world of childhood has a double existence; it is a part of the narrator's past, but it lives within her and thus becomes part of the present. Incidents of the narrator's present life recall analogous incidents of her childhood. The voyage between the present and the past is a constant motif in Colette's works, and as it is usually a concrete object or a physical sensation which recalls the past, the reconstruction of the past is concrete and specific. The

need to find again a once tangible world, to bring it
back to life, is undoubtedly one of the determining factors in Colette's ferocious attachment to the real.

Through the very fact that characters, places, names
and details reappear from novel to novel, from the
third-person writings to the first-person writings, Colette's work has a very particular unity. Renée in *La
Vagabonde* speaks of the incident that is developed in
"Le Képi." May and Jean of *La Vagabonde* reappear, in
a slightly different light, in *Le Pur et l'Impur*; the *fanal
bleu* exists both in *Le Toutounier* and in the long meditation to which it gives its name; the same shawl is used
by the characters in *Duo* and *La Seconde*.

There is always one principal action in Colette's
works, whether they be novels or meditations and reminiscences. This action always involves a loss. And if the
character who has suffered this loss is able to survive,
then through the loss there is a gain, a gain in lucidity,
a gain in knowledge of self. Loss is a new experience, a
further contact with the real.

Colette's characters, with the exception of "Sido" and
"Colette," usually seek happiness and seek it through
love. But there is no permanent happiness in love, indeed there is no possibility of permanent happiness.

It is Sido who taught me that the word happiness does
not have much meaning. Is it, moreover, something indispensable to existence? Generally people would like to make
us think so. But it is not normal that a human being, any
more than an animal, should relish a state that would be
a state of perfect happiness. I do not think a great deal
about happiness, I do not like it a great deal. I do not like
it enough.[23]

In *La Naissance du Jour*, the narrator, "Colette," speaking to her heart says, "You scorned happiness, let us pay ourselves this tribute." [24] Just as Colette refuses any abstract notion about life, so does she refuse to accept as "real" such an absolute term as happiness. This refusal of the facile, accompanied by a strong sense of honor, runs all through Colette's work, in her style as well as in her personal relation to life. Maurice Goudeket quotes her as saying, "One must beware of falling toward the side to which one leans." [25] The difficult equilibrium which the narrator reaches in *La Naissance du Jour*, *L'Etoile Vesper* and *Le Fanal bleu*, the equilibrium which Claudine reaches in *La Retraite sentimentale* and Lèa in *La fin de Chéri*, the equilibrium which "Sido" exemplifies in *La Maison de Claudine* and *Sido*, demands a very special kind of heroism, a renunciation of what is ordinarily thought of as happiness.

> First of all, happiness is a word that has no meaning; there are all kinds of happinesses. But there is no stable happiness; the stability of happiness is an impossible thing. Furthermore, one should not desire happiness; one should build it in the best possible way. . . . Adapt oneself to what life brings, know how to pick up the pieces of a destroyed happiness and stick them together as well as possible so as to make another. And then suppress, energetically, all that is unbearable, or do something about it.[26]

This acceptance of the inevitable implicit in all Colette's works is directly related to her sense of perspective. What happens to a human being is real, it is an incontrovertible truth. One cannot refuse to accept it, any more than one can refuse to see the world in which one lives. The care which goes into the reproduction of an object with words must also go into the arrangement, the piecing together of a human life. Colette's moral imperative is an active one. It demands constant vigilance. One may reach an equilibrium, one may even attain momentary happiness, but at no moment may one be passive. Colette's joy and gratitude in the presence of the richness and the variety of nature is often tinged with a certain sadness. As there is in physical love a subtle blending of pleasure and melancholy so, in the understanding which the narrator "Colette" attains through loss, there is inevitable pain.

Colette—and this, perhaps, is what is most remarkable—is at the same time magician and sage, a master stylist and a wise moralist. "Regarde" is the key to her point of view on this world, and it is also the key to the equilibrium which a human being may reach in this world. For the artist and the non-artist the imperative is the same. There is, in fact, no difference between the way in which the artist must create his work and the way in which the human being must create his life. In the works of Colette and in the life of the narrator "Colette," may be found a perfect fusion of the two. The particular point of view which her art reveals and the equilibrium which she reached in old age are both a result of her complete acceptance of the real, of her desire to depict it in words, of her desire to face it with courage.

Notes

All quotations are from the *Oeuvres complètes de Colette* (Paris, Flammarion, 1948–1950), unless otherwise indicated.

I

1. This refusal caused much comment in France, England and the United States.
2. Henri Peyre, *The Contemporary French Novel* (New York, Oxford University Press, 1955), 283.
3. Julien Benda, *Belphégor* (Paris, Emile-Paul Frères, 1918); Gonzague Truc, *Madame Colette* (Paris, Corrêa, 1941).
4. Jean Cocteau, *Colette* (Paris, Grasset, 1955), 41.
5. The Proust letter is quoted by Claude Chauvière, *Colette* (Paris, Firmin-Didot et Cie., 1931), 146–148. In another letter, also quoted by Claude Chauvière, Proust praises certain descriptions of Venice which appeared in "Impressions d'Italie."
6. *Trait pour Trait*, 194.
7. Chauvière, *Colette*, 148–149.
8. André Gide, *Journal* (Paris, Gallimard, 1939, 1946), February 19, 1936; February 11, 1941.
9. Maurice Goudeket, *Près de Colette* (Paris, Flammarion, 1956), 109. The *Figaro Littéraire* in its special "Hommage à Colette," January

24, 1953, contains the following undated words written by Paul Valéry:

> To Colette,
> who, alone of her sex,
> knows that writing is an art,
> possesses it and puts to shame
> many men who ignore it.
>   Her friend,
>   Paul Valéry.

10. Colette's correspondence with the French Catholic writer, Francis Jammes, published in 1945 with an introduction and notes by Robert Mallet, is an excellent example of her attitude. In 1904, Colette sent Jammes a copy of her *Dialogues de Bêtes*. Jammes both highly praised the work and wrote a preface for it. Their correspondence, which covers a two-year period, 1904–1906, is only superficially literary. In rather vague terms, each praises the works of the other. Their letters are mainly concerned with that which Colette and Jammes held in common—a love of nature.

11. There is a certain similarity between the word *"Regarde"* as used by Colette and the word "Live" as used by Lambert Strether in Henry James's novel, *The Ambassadors* (New York, Harper and Brothers, 1948), 150. Despite James's greater subtlety, both he and Colette use these imperatives to describe a necessary attitude toward life, an attitude which demands that one be alert and receptive to the incidents and impressions of one's experience.

12. Goudeket, *Près de Colette*, 292.

II

1. *La Naissance du Jour*, 89.
2. To date, no complete biography of Colette exists, although Maurice Goudeket is, at present, writing one.
3. For a particularly devastating portrait of Colette, see Sylvain Bonmariage, *Willy, Colette et Moi* (Moulin, Editions Charles Fremanger, La Nouvelle Provence Littéraire, 1954).

III

1. "Jour Gris," *Les Vrilles de la Vigne*, 222.
2. In her fictionalized reminiscences, Colette always refers to her mother as "Sido," never as Sido. This is Colette's way, which has been followed here, of showing the transposition of a real person into fiction.

3. Some of Sido's letters are used in *La Naissance du Jour,* and others have been published in *Le Figaro Littéraire's* "Hommage à Colette," January 24, 1953. For a discussion of these letters, see pp. 211–212.

4. At the time of the German occupation, Colette was to write very moving passages about her country and her love for her country. For example: ". . . je voue à mon pays un culte assoupi au fond de moi-même. Nous fûmes gâtes par la succulence et la grâce de la terre française, chaude dans tous ses plis d'avoir abrité l'être humain. Au tournant de la route, au coin de la rue, sur les plages, en haut de la côte, nous recevions des dons inestimables, monnayés en flots phosphorescents, en pommiers fleuris, en pâturages, en palais historiques, en fruits de la vallée du Rhône. Nous ne savions pas que des coups portés à un si beau pays, nous retentirions tous. Maintenant nous le savons. Il en va de cet amour-là comme de l'autre amour: la joie nous apprend sur lui peu de chose. Nous ne sommes sûrs de sa présence et de sa force que dans la douleur." (". . . I dedicate to my country a cult latent within me. We were spoiled by the succulence and the grace of the French soil, rich in all its hollows from having sheltered the human being. At the turning of the road, at the corner of the street, on the beaches, above the coast, we received inestimable gifts, coined in phosphorescent waves, in flowering apple trees, in pastures, in historic palaces, in fruits from the valley of the Rhône. We did not know that the blows inflicted on so beautiful a country would echo in all of us. Now we know it. It is the same with that love as with the other: joy teaches us little. We are sure of its presence and of its force only in sorrow.") *De ma Fenêtre,* 279–280.

5. "Le Miroir," *Les Vrilles de la Vigne* (Paris, Ferenczi, 1934).

6. Colette's knowledge of animal and plant life was immense. In 1957, while the present author was working in Colette's apartment, her maid Pauline, produced a huge book, *Histoire Naturelle—Les Plantes,* by J. Constantin and F. Fardeau, which Colette often read. The book contains rather involved biological and geographical studies, as well as many pictures.

7. A chapter of *Journal à rebours.*

8. *Ibid.,* 96.

9. *Ibid.,* 97.

10. *Ibid.*

11. This examination is given in France at a level that corresponds roughly to the end of Junior High School in America.

12. "Rêverie de Nouvel An," *Les Vrilles de la Vigne,* 210.

13. *Sido,* 179.

14. *Ibid.,* 461

15. *La Naissance du Jour,* 27.

16. *La Maison de Claudine,* 11.

17. *Sido,* 197.

le la Hire,
spic, 1905);

........., ...c ças vvilly, *Les Samedis littéraires, 5ème série* (Paris, E. Sansot, 1907), 126.
8. J. H. Rosny Aîné, *Portraits et Souvenirs* (Paris, Compagnie Française des Arts Graphiques, 1945), 85.
9. *Mes Apprentissages,* 70.
10. *Ibid.,* 62.
11. Quoted by Le Cardonnel and Vellay, *La Littérature contemporaine* (Paris, Le Mercure de France, 1905), 310.
12. *Mes Apprentissages,* 71.
13. *Ibid.*
14. Willy, *Souvenirs littéraires et autres* (Paris, Editions Montaigne, 1925), titles of Chapters I, II and V.
15. *Les Lettres de l'Ouvreuse* was a series of articles on music which Willy, with the help of two musicologists, Alfred Ernest and Emile Vuillermoz, "wrote" for the newspaper *L'Echo de Paris.* It has been suggested that Willy was occasionally aided by Colette. The tone of these articles, supposedly written by an usher (*l'Ouvreuse*), is reminiscent of the tone of *Souvenirs littéraires et autres.* They deal with the concerts and operas which Willy attended. The composer most often mentioned by Willy is Wagner. Monsieur Willy was a great Wagner enthusiast, and he was one of the first to publicize the works of the German composer and his disciples in France, where hitherto Wagner had been admired by a small elite. Although Willy's understanding of and love for Wagner are genuine, there is an underlying refusal on his part to be anything but jovial and cynical, and, one might add, vulgar. It seems as though Willy would do or write almost anything in order to be known.
16. Willy, *Suzette veut me lâcher* (Paris, Librairie Nelson, n.d.).
17. *Mes Apprentissages,* 59–60.
18. *Ibid.,* 35.
19. *La Vagabonde,* 30.
20. *Mes Apprentissages,* 26
21. *Ibid.,* 117–118.

22. *Ibid.*, 33.
23. *Ibid.*
24. *Ibid.*, 69.
25. *Ibid.*, 81.
26. *Trois . . . Six . . . Neuf . . .*, 475.
27. *Mes Apprentissages*, 123.
28. *Lettres à Hélène Picard*, 62–63.
29. In the two available recordings of Colette's voice, made when she was quite advanced in age, her voice, while very rich, is indeed grumbling and even booming.

V

1. *La Naissance du Jour*, 7.
2. "Claudine" here refers to the Claudine of *La Maison de Claudine*, not to the Claudine of the *Claudine* novels.
3. "Sido" here refers to the Sido of *Sido* and *La Maison de Claudine*.

VI

1. This is attributed by Colette to one of her husbands. *La Naissance du Jour*, 18–19.
2. *Hommage à Colette* (Les Editions de l'Imprimerie de Monaco, n.d.). There is no pagination in this book, which contains the speech read by Colette at the first film showing of *Le Blé en herbe*, to a student audience.
3. Frédéric Lefèvre, "Une heure avec Colette," *Les Nouvelles Littéraires*, March 27, 1926.
4. Note two of her titles: *La Seconde* (1929), referring to the second in a duel, and *Duo* (1934).
5. For a discussion of *La Chatte*, see pp. 190–193.
6. *Le Pur et l'Impur*, 25.
7. These novels have been adapted as plays: *La Vagabonde, Chéri Gigi, Duo, La Seconde*; these, as films: *Claudine à l'Ecole, L'Ingénue libertine, Mitsou, Le Blé en herbe, Julie de Carneilhan, La Chatte, Gigi.*

VII

1. *Mes Apprentissages*, 57–58.
2. *Ibid.*, 58–59.
3. Willy was undoubtedly hoping that his wife would write a novel that would be as successful as Liane de Pougy's *L'Insaisissable*, published

in Paris by the Librairie Nelson, 1898. In this novel, a famous and unhappy courtesan receives a visit from her first lover. The novel then becomes the story of their love affair, told through their correspondence. The last line, "Nothing in this world is worth a kiss," sums up the tone, the atmosphere, and the subject of this rather dull story.

4.. This was a famous eighteenth-century novel by Choderlos de Laclos, infinitely superior to *Claudine à l'Ecole*.

5. *Mes Apprentissages*, 46. This conversation between Colette and Catulle Mendès took place in the office of *L'Echo de Paris*, probably in 1904.

6. "Le Miroir," *Les Vrilles de la Vigne* (Paris, Ferenczi, 1934), 187.

7. *Claudine à l'Ecole*, 165.

8. Claudine is almost as ubiquitous as the narrator of *A la Recherche du temps perdu*.

9. The original manuscript of *Claudine à l'Ecole* no longer exists. It would have been a most revealing document.

10. Simone de Beauvoir's novel, *L'Invitée*, is, as Jean Cocteau has amusingly remarked, a kind of existentialist paraphrase of *Claudine en Ménage*. Another of Colette's novels, *La Seconde*, is even closer in theme to *L'Invitée*.

11. *Casamène* is a literary transposition of *Les Monts Boucons*, the house surrounded by a small farm, in Franche-Comté, which Willy temporarily gave to Colette and where, in a *"solitude surveillée"* she often worked.

12. Although the *Dialogues de Bêtes* (1904), the first of her works which Colette was to sign, falls chronologically into this first period of Colette's literary activity, a later chapter will deal with Colette's animal stories and their importance in her work. It is sufficient to note here that the *Dialogues* represents a return to the world of nature and a withdrawal from the world of men which is transposed into fiction at the end of *La Retraite sentimentale*. The first edition of the *Dialogues de Bêtes* bears the epigraph, *"Pour amuser Willy."*

13. *Mes Apprentissages*, 82.

14.. Preface to *L'Ingénue libertine*, 7.

15. See the opening line of *Suzette veut me lâcher*, quoted on p. 32.

VIII

1. Preface to *La Vagabonde*, 5.

2. *Ibid.*

3. Renée's mime partner is called "Braque," an obvious transformation of the name of Colette's partner, Georges Wague.

4. One is tempted, in this connection, to make a comparison with Michel Butor's novel, *La Modification*.
5. This was written nine years before Paul Valéry's famous poem, "Le Cimetière marin," which has as its setting the cemetery by the sea of the town of Sète.
6. *La Vagabonde*, 208.
7. *Ibid.*, 223.
8. *Ibid.*
9. *Ibid.*
10. *Ibid.*

IX

1. *Gigi*, 14.
2. *Ibid.*, 10.
3. Proust to Colette, quoted in Claude Chauvière, *Colette* (Paris, Firmin-Didot et Compagnie, 1931), 146–148.
4. *Gigi*, 28.
5. *Mitsou*, 202.

X

1. *Bella-Vista*, 171.
2. *La Seconde*, 137.
3. Colette's unmarried brother, Léo Colette, is very likely the principal model for Léon de Carneilhan.
4. *La Seconde*, 188.
5. *Ibid.*, 244.
6. *Duo*, 330.
7. *Ibid.*, 300.
8. *Le Toutounier*, 363.
9. *Ibid.*, 420.
10. *Ibid.*, 361.
11. *Julie de Carneilhan*, 149.
12. *Ibid.*, 154.

XI

1. The author is indebted to Richard Hayes, "Wisdom of Colette," *Commonweal*, September 5, 1952, for this title. Mr. Hayes refers to Colette's "greatest gift" as "the ability to create parables of experi-

ence, with the conciseness, the exact *correspondence of image and idea, of the finest poetry.*"

2. *Le Blé en herbe,* 330.

3. André Parinaud, "Dialogue avec Colette," *Revue des Hommes et des Mondes,* February, 1953.

4. These early versions have been collected under the title of "Clouk et Chéri," in *Mes Cahiers.*

5. Frédéric Lefèvre, "Une heure avec Colette," *Les Nouvelles Littéraires,* March 27, 1926.

6. *Chéri,* 13.

7. *Ibid.,* 17.

8. *La fin de Chéri,* 222.

9. *Chéri,* 39.

10. *Ibid.,* 29. In *Près de Colette,* Monsieur Goudeket quotes Colette as uttering much the same words.

11. *Chéri,* 105.

12. *Ibid.,* 127.

13. *Ibid.,* 136.

14. *Ibid.,* 137.

15. *Ibid.*

16. *Ibid.,* 156.

17. *La fin de Chéri,* 161.

18. *Ibid.,* 204.

19. *Ibid.,* 256.

20. *Ibid.,* 284.

21. Parinaud, "Dialogue avec Colette."

22. *Hommage à Colette.*

23. Thanks to Monsieur Goudeket, the author was able to see an early manuscript of *Le Blé en herbe.*

24. *Le Blé en herbe,* 256.

25. Longus, *Daphnis et Chloë,* translated by Amyot, revised by Paul Louis Courier (Paris, Librairie Alphonse Lemerre, 1928).

26. See p. 147 and the comparison made by Colette between Philippe and Daphnis.

27. *Le Blé en herbe,* 256.

28. *Ibid.,* 268.

29. *Ibid.,* 353.

30. *Ibid.,* 346–347.

XII

1. "Châ," *La Femme cachée,* 456.

2. "L'Enfant malade" was published for the first time with *Gigi,* in 1945, although the story was written at an unknown, earlier date.

3. "La Femme cachée," *La Femme cachée*, 375.
4. "L'Aube," *ibid.*, 380.
5. "La Main," *ibid.*, 389.
6. "L'Impasse," *ibid.*, 393.
7. "Le Juge," *ibid.*, 402.
8. "Le Cambrioleur," *ibid.*, 421.
9. "L'Habitude," *ibid.*, 469.
10. "L'Assassin," *ibid.*, 432.
11. "Le Paysage," *ibid.*, 441.
12. "La Femme cachée," *ibid.*, 379.
13. "Le rendez-vous," *Bella-Vista*, 269.
14. "L'Enfant malade," *Gigi*, 64.
15. *Ibid.*, 72.

XIII

1. *La Jumelle noire*, 362.
2. Colette speaks of working on other adaptations, but these adaptations have never been published and were perhaps never completed. Since Colette did not read English well, Maurice Goudeket did a first translation from which she worked. *Le Ciel de Lit* (*The Four Poster Bed*) by Jan de Hartog is an amusing comedy about the successive stages in the marital life of a couple. The subject is obviously one which would have interested Colette.
3. *En Camarades*, 258.
4. *La Jumelle noire*, 125.
5. *Chéri*, 14.
6. *La Décapitée*, 294.
7. *L'Enfant et les Sortilèges*, 318.
8. *Ibid.*, 317.
9. *Ibid.*, 324.
10. *Ibid.*, 329–330.
11. *La Jumelle noire*, 35.
12. *Ibid.*, 212.
13. *Ibid.*, 248.

XIV

1. *Le Fanal bleu*, 8.
2. In subsequent editions of *Les Vrilles de la Vigne*, new chapters were added and original ones omitted. This discussion deals only with those chapters which appeared in the 1908 edition.
3. "Les Vrilles de la Vigne," *Les Vrilles de la Vigne*, 207. This quota-

tion may be compared to a similar one in *La Naissance du Jour*, 56.

4. *Trois* . . . *Six* . . . *Neuf* . . . is the title of a play written by Michel Duran and reviewed by Colette on February 9, 1936, *La Jumelle noire*, 313. Colette speaks in her review of "valises opened as soon as they are closed," and this perhaps accounts for the similarity in the titles.

5. *L'Etoile Vesper*, 303.

6. "Nuit Blanche," *Les Vrilles de la Vigne*, 218.

7. *Ibid.*, 220.

8. *Bella-Vista*, 133.

9. "La Dame du Photographe," *Gigi*, 129.

XV

1. Quoted by Maurice Goudeket, *Près de Colette* (Paris, Flammarion, 1956), 35. Colette and her husband had gone to see a film about flowers. This may have been an echo of Balzac's "Il n'y a qu'un animal," in the foreword to the *Comédie humaine*.

2. Goudeket, *Près de Colette*, 35.

3. *De ma Fenêtre*, 376.

4. The one writer of animal stories mentioned in Colette's work is Rudyard Kipling. In *Claudine à l'Ecole*, Claudine speaks of "animal stories, marvelously related by Rudyard Kipling (there's a man who knows animals)." (p. 126) And in "Bel-Gazou et la vie chère," in *Les Heures longues*, Colette reads to her daughter a Kipling story "in which the animals speak." (p. 285)

5. *Claudine en Ménage*, 107.

6. "Ma Mère et les Bêtes," *La Maison de Claudine*, 53.

7. *Sido*, 187.

8. "Le Coeur des Bêtes," *Journal à rebours*.

9. In reading through Colette's novels and short stories, one discovers about four hundred such analogies. They are even more frequent in her first-person writings. One of the best examples may be found in *De ma Fenêtre*. Colette is describing wartime children overcome by sleep in the early morning, and she uses both animal and plant imagery: "Their heads bent, they return to the unfinished dream, curl themselves up in their own manner, which is also, toward the end of the night, the manner of the cat rolled like a turban, of the pigeon with his head on his breast, of the bent back end of the fern, of the sensitive petals of the anemone." (p. 293)

10. *Claudine à l'Ecole*, 141.

11. "Bâ-tou," *La Maison de Claudine*, 141.

12. "Amours," *Les Vrilles de la Vigne*. 294.

13. *Ibid.*, 295.

14. *La Chatte*, 145.
15. *Ibid.*, 151.
16. *Ibid.*, 149.
17. *Ibid.*, 156.
18. *Ibid.*, 160.
19. *Ibid.*, 161.
20. *Ibid.*
21. *Ibid.*, 170.
22. *Mes Apprentissages*, 82.
23. In *De ma Fenêtre*, Colette comments on the fact that animals know more about humans than do humans about animals: "For all animals very quickly know a great deal about us, while we still ignore the rudiments of their ordinary language, the meaning of their lamentations and their chants." (p. 317)
24. "Fleurs," *La Treille Muscate*, 332.
25. *Flore et Pomone*, 132.
26. *Ibid.*, 133.
27. "Rose," *Pour un Herbier*, 142.
28. "Orchidée," *Pour un Herbier*, 150.
29. *Ibid.*
30. *Ibid.*, 151.
31. *Ibid.*, 150.
32. *Ibid.*, 148–149.

XVI

1. *La Naissance du Jour*, 56.
2. *Sido*, 174.
3. One might question the order chosen by Colette and Maurice Goudeket in the *Oeuvres complètes* for the distribution of those "Sido-childhood" stories which are not included either in *La Maison de Claudine* or in *Sido*. Such chapters as "Un Zouave" in *Les Heures longues*, "Progéniture" in *Adventures quotidiennes*, "Le Sieur Bernard" in *Bella-Vista*, "Sido et Moi" and "La Chaufferette" in *Journal à rebours*, "La Cire verte" in *Le Képi*, "Des Mères, des Enfants . . ." and "Noël ancien" in *La Fleur de l'Age*, even though they were written at different periods, could profitably have been placed together and in the same volume as *La Maison de Claudine* and *Sido*.
4. *La Maison de Claudine*, 10.
5. *Ibid.*, 28–29.
6. Frédéric Lefèvre, "Une Heure avec Colette."
7. The same question that has been raised concerning the distribution of "Sido-childhood" stories applies to the Bel-Gazou stories. They are scattered under the following titles: "Regarde" in *Autres Bêtes*, "Bel-

Gazou et Buck" in *La Paix chez les Bêtes*, "Bel-Gazou et la Guerre" and "Bel-Gazou et la vie chère" in *Les Heures longues*, "La Chambre éclairée," "Fantômes," "Conte de Bel-Gazou à sa poupée" and "Bel-Gazou et le cinéma" in *La Chambre éclairée*.

8. Anatole France uses this same double perspective in *Le Livre de mon Ami*, as does Marcel Proust, but with greater complexity, in *A la Recherche du temps perdu*.

9. *La Maison de Claudine*, 24.

10. *Ibid.*, 57.

11. *Ibid.*, 79.

12. *Ibid.*, 124.

13. See pp. 211–212 for a discussion of Sido's letters.

14. See Chapter XVII for a more complete discussion of this manuscript.

15. "Le Capitaine," *Sido*, 209–210.

16. "Sido," *ibid.*, 191.

17. "Le Capitaine," *ibid.*, 199.

18. *Ibid.*, 201.

19. *Mes Apprentissages*, 66.

20. "Fantômes," *La Chambre éclairée*, 393.

21. "Bel-Gazou et la vie chère," *Les Heures longues*, 341.

22. "La Noisette creuse," *La Maison de Claudine*, 170.

23. *Ibid.*

24. The words which compose this title appear in "Ma Mère et le Fruit Defendu," *La Maison de Claudine*, 132. Sido's early-morning activities continued even after she was past seventy and ill. ". . . she always managed to live her best moments in independence before the earliest risers had opened their shutters, and she could tell us of the cats' awakening, of the events in the nests, of the news brought by the milkmaid with the milk and the baker's girl with the bread, the chronicle of the birth of a new day."

25. In the preface to *La Maison de Claudine*, 7, Colette writes, "*La Naissance du Jour* gave me the occasion to glorify her letters and to be proud of them."

26. These letters may also be found in the English edition of *My Mother's House* and *Sido*.

27. In *Positions et Propositions* (Paris, Gallimard, 1928), 78, Paul Claudel makes a comment about style which is very relevant here: ". . . style is a natural quality like the sound of the voice, it is by no means the appanage of professional writers. In the letters of Isabelle Rimbaud we find a muffled echo of the fraternal instrument, and perhaps the great writer only realizes a certain tone slowly elaborated and ripened by a family." And Claudel adds a footnote, "In the same way today Madame Colette and her mother."

28. "Hommage à Colette," *Le Figaro Littéraire*. The date of the letter is April 1, 1904.

29. December 30, 1911. *Ibid.*
30. *La Naissance du Jour*, 56.
31. *Ibid.*, 19.
32. *Ibid.*, 7.
33. *Ibid.*, 13, 18.
34. This was not the only time that Colette was to anticipate the future. In *L'Enfant malade*, Colette explores the dreams and fantasies of a child who is ill and unable to move. Her own immobility, due to her severe arthritis, is thus anticipated. (See Maurice Goudeket, *Près de Colette* [Paris, Flammarion, 1956].)
35. *La Naissance du Jour*, 14.
36. *Ibid.*, 33.
37. *Ibid.*, 99.
38. *Ibid.*, 23.
39. *Ibid.*, 22.
40. *Ibid.*, 24.
41. *Ibid.*, 99.
42. *Ibid.*, 47.
43. Originally published in 1932, under the title *Ces Plaisirs*. The definitive edition, under the title *Le Pur et l'Impur*, was published in 1941.
44. *Le Pur et l'Impur*, 137.
45. *La Naissance du Jour*, 25.
46. *Ibid.*
47. *Ibid.*
48. *Le Pur et l'Impur*, 137.
49. *Ibid.*, 136.
50. *Ibid.*, 93.
51. *Ibid.* 119.
52. *Ibid.*, 100–101.
53. *Ibid.*, 118.

XVII

1. *Sido*, 187.
2. *De ma Fenêtre*, 335.
3. Claude Roy, "Classique Colette," *Colette, Point*, May, 1951.
4. Paul Reboux, *Colette ou le génie du Style* (Paris, Rasmussen, 1925), 60.
5. Henry de Montherlant, quoted in Germaine Beaumont and André Parinaud, eds., *Colette par elle-même* (Paris, Editions du Seuil, 1956), 191.
6. Henri Peyre, *The Contemporary French Novel* (New York, Oxford University Press, 1955), 282.

7. Maria Le Hardouin, *Colette* (Paris, Editions Universitaires, 1956), 102.
8. A detailed study of Colette's style would, in itself, require more than one volume, the use of a very technical vocabulary, and abundant quotations, which, translated, would be quite meaningless. It is not the intention here to engage in such a study, but rather to indicate the most important aspects of the relationship between what and how Colette wrote.
9. A manuscript which, thanks to the kindness of Maurice Goudeket, the present author was able to study at leisure in Colette's Palais Royal apartment. The manuscript was carefully covered with a piece of an old blue dress with white flowers which belonged to Sido.
10. *Sido*, 182.
11. "Fleurs," *Mélanges*, 335.
12. *L'Etoile Vesper*, 238.
13. *Ibid.*, 189.
14. André Parinaud, "Dialogue avec Colette," *Revue des Hommes et des Mondes*, February, 1953.
15. *Ibid.*
16. "Le Dernier Feu," *Les Vrilles de la Vigne*, 226.
17. *La Naissance du Jour*, 67.
18. *Ibid.*, 62.
19. André Gide, "Hommage à Colette," *Colette, Point*, May, 1951, 4.
20. "Salon d'Automne," *La Paix chez les Bêtes*, 301.
21. *De ma Fenêtre*, 335.
22. "Préface: à *Aux Iles de la Lumière*, par Renée Hamon," *Mélanges*, 371. This book was originally published by Flammarion in 1939.
23. Parinaud, "Dialogue avec Colette." The quotation refers both to Sido and animals, the two main sources of Colette's own attitude toward life.
24. *La Naissance du Jour*, 30.
25. Maurice Goudeket, *Près de Colette* (Paris, Flammarion, 1956), 31.
26. M. Romain, "De quoi le bonheur est-il fait?" Interview with Colette, *Les Annales*, March 25, 1937.

Bibliography

WORKS BY COLETTE

For a complete bibliography of Colette's published writings see the *Oeuvres complètes de Colette* and Elaine Marks, "Colette: A Critical Study" (doctoral thesis, New York University, 1957).

Oeuvres complètes de Colette. Paris, Flammarion, 1948–1950. This definitive edition of Colette's works is being translated and published in England by Secker and Warburg and distributed in the United States by Farrar, Straus and Cudahy.

Volume I: *Claudine à l'Ecole, Claudine à Paris.*
Volume II: *Claudine en Ménage, Claudine s'en va, La Retraite sentimentale.*
Volume III: *L'Ingénue libertine, Les Vrilles de la Vigne, Douze Dialogues de Bêtes, Autres Bêtes.*
Volume IV: *La Vagabonde, L'Entrave, Dans la Foule.*
Volume V: *L'Envers du Music-Hall, Mitsou, La Paix chez les Bêtes, Les Heures longues, La Chambre éclairée.*
Volume VI: *Chéri, La fin de Chéri, Le Voyage égoïste, Aventures quotidiennes.*
Volume VII: *La Maison de Claudine, Sido, Noces, Le Blé en herbe, La Femme cachée.*

Volume VIII: *La Naissance du Jour, La Seconde, Prisons et Paradis, Nudité.*
Volume IX: *Le Pur et l'Impur, La Chatte, Duo, Le Toutounier, Belles Saisons.*
Volume X: *La Jumelle noire.*
Volume XI: *Mes Apprentissages, Bella-Vista, Chambre d'Hôtel, Julie de Carneilhan.*
Volume XII: *Journal à rebours, Le Képi, De ma Fenêtre, Trois . . . Six . . . Neuf . . .*
Volume XIII: *Gigi, L'Etoile Vesper, Mes Cahiers, Discours de réception.*
Volume XIV: *Le Fanal bleu, Pour un Herbier, Trait pour Trait, Journal intermittent, La Fleur de l'Age, En Pays connu, A Portée de la main.*
Volume XV: *Théâtre: Chéri, La Vagabonde, En Camarades, La Décapitée, L'Enfant et les Sortilèges. Mélanges, Bibliographie.*

WORKS BY COLETTE IN ORDER OF PUBLICATION

(The titles of the English editions are, in each case, those of the most recent translations.)

Claudine à l'Ecole. Paris, P. Ollendorf, 1900. (*Claudine at School.* Translated by Antonia White. New York, Farrar, Straus and Cudahy, 1957.)
Claudine à Paris. Paris, P. Ollendorf, 1901. (*Claudine in Paris.* Translated by Antonia White. New York, Farrar, Straus and Cudahy, 1958.)
Claudine en Ménage. Paris, Mercure de France, 1902. (*The Indulgent Husband.* Translated by Frederick A. Blossom. New York, Rinehart and Company, 1935.)
Claudine s'en va. Paris, P. Ollendorf, 1903. (*The Innocent Wife.* Translated by Frederick A. Blossom. New York, Farrar and Rinehart, 1934.)
Minne. Paris, P. Ollendorf, 1904.
Les égarements de Minne. Paris, P. Ollendorf, 1905.
Dialogues de Bêtes. Paris, Mercure de France, 1904. (See: *Creatures Great and Small.* Translated by Enid McLeod. New York, Farrar, Straus and Cudahy, 1957.)
Sept Dialogues de Bêtes. Préface de Francis Jammes. Paris, Mercure de France, 1905. (See: *Creatures Great and Small.*)
La Retraite sentimentale. Paris, Mercure de France, 1907.
Les Vrilles de la Vigne. Paris, Editions de la Vie Parisienne, 1908.
L'Ingénue libertine. Paris, P. Ollendorf, 1909. (*The Gentle Libertine.*

Translated by R.C.B. New York, Farrar and Rinehart, 1931.)

La Vagabonde. Paris, P. Ollendorf, 1911. (*The Vagabond.* Translated by Enid McLeod. New York, Farrar, Straus and Young, 1955.)

L'Envers du Music-Hall. Paris, Flammarion, 1913. (*Music-Hall Sidelights.* Translated by Anna-Marie Callimachi. New York, Farrar, Straus and Cudahy, 1958.)

L'Entrave. Paris, Librairie des Lettres, 1913. (*Recaptured.* Translated by Viola Gerard Garvin. New York, Cosmopolitan Book Corporation, 1931.)

Prrou, Poucette et quelques autres. Paris, Librairie des Lettres, 1913.

La Paix chez les Bêtes. Paris, A. Fayard, 1916. The first ten stories are a new edition of *Prrou, Poucette et quelques autres.* (See: *Creatures Great and Small.*)

Les Heures longues. Paris, A. Fayard, 1914–1917.

Les Enfants dans les Ruines. Paris, Editions de la Maison du Livre, 1917.

Dans la Foule. Paris, Editions Georges Crès et Cie., 1918.

Mitsou ou comment l'esprit vient aux Filles. Paris, A. Fayard, 1919. This edition also contains *En Camarades, pièce en deux actes.* (*Mitsou.* Translated by Raymond Postgate. New York, Farrar, Straus and Cudahy, 1958.)

La Chambre éclairée. Paris, Edouard Joseph, 1920.

Chéri. Paris, A. Fayard, 1920. (*Chéri* and *The Last of Chéri.* Translated by Roger Senhouse. New York, Farrar, Straus and Young, 1953.)

La Maison de Claudine. Paris, J. Ferenczi et fils, 1922. (*My Mother's House* and *Sido.* Translated by Enid McLeod and Una Troubridge. New York, Farrar, Straus and Young, 1953.)

Le Voyage égoïste. Paris, Editions d'art Edouard Pelletan, 1922.

Chéri, comédie en quatre actes, par Colette et Léopold Marchand. Paris, Librairie Théâtrale, 1922. (*Chéri.* Adapted for the stage by Anita Loos, based on the novels *Chéri* and *The Last of Chéri,* 1959.)

Le Blé en herbe. Paris, Flammarion, 1923. (*The Ripening Seed.* Translated by Roger Senhouse. New York, Farrar, Straus and Cudahy, 1956.)

Rêverie de Nouvel An. Paris, Stock, 1925.

La Femme cachée. Paris, Flammarion, 1924.

Adventures quotidiennes. Paris, Flammarion, 1924.

Quatre Saisons. Paris, Philippe Ortiz, 1925.

L'Enfant et les Sortilèges. Musique de Maurice Ravel. Paris, Durand et Cie., 1925.

La fin de Chéri. Paris, Flammarion, 1926. (*Chéri* and *The Last of Chéri.* Translated by Roger Senhouse. New York, Farrar, Straus and Young, 1953.)

La Naissance du Jour. Paris, Flammarion, 1928. (*A Lesson in Love.* Translated by Rosemary Benêt. New York, Farrar and Rinehart, 1932.)

Renée Vivien. Abbeville, F. Paillart, 1928.

La Seconde. Paris, J. Ferenczi et fils, 1929. (*The Other One.* Translated by Viola Gerard Garvin. New York, Cosmopolitan Book Corporation, 1931.)

Sido. Paris, Editions Krâ, 1929. (*My Mother's House* and *Sido.* Translated by Enid McLeod and Una Troubridge. New York, Farrar, Straus and Young, 1953.)

Histoires pour Bel-Gazou. Paris, Stock, 1930.

Douze Dialogues de Bêtes. Paris, Mercure de France, 1930. (See: *Creatures Great and Small.*)

Paradis terrestres. Lausanne, Gonin et Cie., 1932.

La Treille Muscate. Paris, Aimé Jourde, 1932.

Prisons et Paradis. Paris, J. Ferenczi et fils, 1932.

Ces Plaisirs. Paris, J. Ferenczi et fils, 1932. (In the 1941 edition, the title was changed to *Le Pur et l'Impur.*

La Chatte. Paris, Bernard Grasset, 1933. (*The Cat.* Translated by Antonia White. Included in *7 by Colette.* Introduction by Janet Flanner. New York, Farrar, Straus and Cudahy, 1955.)

Duo. Paris, J. Ferenczi et fils, 1934. (*Duo.* Translated by Frederick A. Blossom. New York, Farrar and Rinehart, 1935.)

La Jumelle noire. Paris, J. Ferenczi et fils, 1934–1938.

Discours de réception à l'Académie Royale de Belgique. Paris, Bernard Grasset, 1936.

Mes Apprentissages. Paris, J. Ferenczi et fils, 1936. (*My Apprenticeship.* Translated by Helen Beauclerk. London, Secker and Warburg, 1957.)

Chats. Paris, Jacques Nam, 1936.

Splendeur des Papillons. Paris, Plon, 1937.

Bella-Vista. Paris, J. Ferenczi et fils, 1937. (See: "Bella-Vista," "Gribiche," "The Rendezvous" and "The Patriarch" in *The Tender Shoot and Other Stories.* Translated by Antonia White. New York, Farrar, Straus and Cudahy, 1959.)

Le Toutounier. Paris, J. Ferenczi et fils, 1939.

Chambre d'Hôtel. Paris, A. Fayard, 1940. (*Chance Acquaintances.* Translated by Patrick Leigh Fermor. Included in *7 by Colette.* "The Rainy Moon." Translated by Antonia White. Included in *The Tender Shoot and Other Stories.*)

Mes Cahiers. Paris, Aux Armes de France, 1941. (This volume includes the four *Cahiers de Colette* which had appeared from 1935 to 1936 in limited editions. The second *Cahier,* 1935, contains "La Décapitée.")

Journal à rebours. Paris, A. Fayard, 1941.

Julie de Carneilhan. Paris, A. Fayard, 1941. (*Julie de Carneilhan.* Translated by Patrick Leigh Fermor. Included in *Gigi, Chance Acquaintances* and *Julie de Carneilhan.* New York, Farrar, Straus and Cudahy, 1952.)

De ma Fenêtre. Paris, Aux Armes de France, 1942.

De la Patte à l'Aile. Paris, Corrêa, 1943.

Flore et Pomone. Paris, Editions de la Galerie Charpentier, 1943.

Nudité. Paris, Editions de la Mappemonde, 1943.

Le Képi. Paris, A. Fayard, 1944. (See: "The Tender Shoot," "The Kepi," "Green Sealing-Wax" and "Armande" in *The Tender Shoot and Other Stories.*)

Broderie ancienne. Monaco, Editions du Rocher, 1944.

Gigi et autres nouvelles. Lausanne, La Guilde du Livre, 1944. (*Gigi.* Translated by Roger Senhouse. Included in *Gigi, Chance Acquaintances* and *Julie de Carneilhan.* New York, Farrar, Straus and Cudahy, 1952 ("The Sick Child" and "The Photographer's Missus." Included in *The Tender Shoot and Other Stories.*)

Trois . . . Six . . . Neuf . . . Paris, Corrêa, 1944.

Belles Saisons. Paris, Editions de la Galerie Charpentier, 1945.

Une Amitié inattendue. Correspondance de Colette et de Francis Jammes. Introduction et notes de Robert Mallet. Paris, Editions Emile-Paul frères, 1945.

L'Etoile Vesper. Genève, Editions du Milieu du Monde, 1946.

Pour un Herbier. Lausanne, Mermod, 1948.

Trait pour Trait. Paris, Editions Le Fleuron, 1949.

Journal intermittent. Paris, Editions Le Fleuron, 1949.

Le Fanal bleu. Paris, J. Ferenczi et fils, 1949.

La Fleur de l'Age. Paris, Editions Le Fleuron, 1949.

En Pays connu. Paris, Editions Manuel Bruker, 1949.

Chats de Colette. Paris, Albin Michel, 1949.

Le Ciel de Lit. Comédie par Jan de Hartog. Adaptation française de Colette. France Illustration, Supplément théâtral et littéraire, no. 144, 1953.

Gigi. Adapté pour la scène par Colette et Anita Loos. France Illustration, Supplément théâtral et littéraire, 1954. (*Gigi.* Dramatized by Anita Loos. New York, Random House, 1952.)

Paysages et Portraits. Paris, Flammarion, 1958.

Lettres à Hélène Picard. Paris, Flammarion, 1958.

"Les Lettres intimes à la confidente Marguerite Moreno," *Le Figaro Littéraire,* July 25–August 8, 1959.

WORKS ON COLETTE: A SELECTED
BIBLIOGRAPHY

An extensive bibliography of works on Colette may be found in Elaine Marks, "Colette: A Critical Study" (doctoral thesis, New York University, 1957).

BOOKS

Boncompain, Claude. *Colette.* Lyon, Confluences, 1944.

Bonmariage, Sylvain. *Willy, Colette et Moi.* Paris, Editions Charles Fremanger, 1954.

Chauvière, Claude. *Colette,* Paris, Firmin-Didot, 1931.

Cocteau, Jean. *Colette.* Paris, Grasset, 1955.

Crosland, Margaret. *Madame Colette. A Provincial in Paris.* London, Peter Owen Ltd., 1953.

Goudeket, Maurice. *Près de Colette.* Paris, Flammarion, 1956. (*Close to Colette.* Translated by Enid McLeod. New York, Farrar, Straus and Cudahy, 1957.)

Larnac, Jean. *Colette, sa vie, son oeuvre.* Paris, Simon Krâ, 1927.

Le Hardouin, Maria. *Colette.* Paris, Editions Universitaires, 1956.

Maulnier, Thierry. *Introduction à Colette.* Paris, La Palme, 1954.

Reboux, Paul. *Colette ou le génie du style.* Paris, Rasmussen, 1925.

Sigl, Robert. *Colette.* Paris, Belles Lettres, 1924.

Trahard, Pierre. *L'Art de Colette.* Paris, Jean Renard, 1941.

Truc, Gonzague. *Madame Colette.* Paris, Corrêa, 1941.

REVIEWS OF WHICH AN ENTIRE ISSUE IS DEVOTED TO COLETTE

Bulletin de l'Iinstitut Français en Espagne. no. 79.

Le Capitole. December 22, 1924.

Le Figaro Littéraire. February 24, 1953.

Hommage à Colette. Editions de l'Imprimerie Nationale de Monaco, 1955.

Lettres Françaises. August 12–19, 1954.

Point. May, 1951.

ARTICLES, CHAPTERS AND PREFACES

Aury, Dominique. "Colette ou le gynécée," *La Nouvelle Revue Française,* March, 1953, pp. 505–511.

Aury, Dominique. "Le Masque du Bonheur," *Arche,* October, 1945.

Beaumont, Germaine. "Présentation," *Colette par elle-même.* Paris, Editions du Seuil, 1956, pp. 5–50.

Brasillach, Robert. "La Sagesse de Colette," *L'Action Française,* August 14, 1930.

Brennan, M. "Books! The Need of Love," *The New Yorker*, January 5, 1952.

Caillot, G. "Sido, Claudine et Colette ne sont plus," *France Illustration*, September, 1954.

Charpentier, J. "La Naissance du Jour," *Le Mercure de France*, June 1, 1928.

Crémieux, Benjamin. "Le Blé en herbe," *Les Nouvelles Littéraires*, August 25, 1923.

Criticus. "Le Style au microscope," *La Revue Mondiale*, August, 1929.

Dumay, Raymond. "Paradoxes de Colette," *Preuves*, September, 1954.

Fernandez, Raymond. "Colette," *La Nouvelle Revue Française*, March 1, 1942.

Flanner, Janet. "Introduction," *7 by Colette*. New York, Farrar, Straus and Cudahy, 1955.

Frish-Fuglsang, Irène. "Le Style de Colette," *Orbis Litterarum*, 1945, no. III; 1946, no. IV.

Gascar, Pierre. "Colette, ou la littérature du don," *Gazette de Lausanne*, August 14–15, 1954.

Greene, Graham. "Lettre au Cardinal Archevêque de Paris," *Le Figaro Littéraire*. August 14, 1954.

Hayes, Richard. "Wisdom of Colette," *Commonweal*, September 5, 1952.

Jammes, Francis. "Préface," *Sept Dialogues de Bêtes*. Paris, Mercure de France, 1905.

Lalane, Louis (Guillaume Apollinaire). "Colette, Willy et Lucie Delarue-Madrus," *Les Marges*, March, 1909.

Lefèvre, Frédéric, *Une Heure Avec . . . 4ème série*, Paris, Gallimard, 1927, pp. 129–142. Reprinted from *Les Nouvelles Littéraires*, March 27, 1926.

Marcel, Gabriel. "Duo," *Europe Nouvelle*, January 12, 1935.

Maulnier, Thierry. "Julie de Carneilhan," *Revue Universelle*, February, 1942.

Mauriac, François. "Dramaturges," *Cahiers d'Occident*, no. 5., pp. 112–114.

Mauriac, François. "Le Roman," *Cahiers de la Quinzaine*. Paris, L'Artisan du Livre, 1928, p. 26.

Pagès, G. "Colette ou le Miracle," *La Grande Revue*, March, 1929.

Parinaud, André. "Dialogue avec Colette," *Revue des Hommes et des Mondes*, February, 1954.

Phelps, R. "Genius of Colette, An Appreciation," *The New Republic*, September 6, 1954.

Pourrat, H. "Le Blé en herbe," *La Nouvelle Revue Française*, September 1, 1923.

Romain, M. "De quoi le bonheur est-il fait?" (Interview with Colette), *Les Annales*, March 25, 1937.

Roy, Claude. "De Claudine à Colette," *Lettres Françaises*, no. 194, 1948.

Roy, Claude. *Descriptions critiques.* Paris, Gallimard, 1949, pp. 107–118.

Roy, Claude. "Classique Colette," *Point*, May, 1951.

Roy, Jean H. "De Colette Willy à Madame Colette," *Les Temps Modernes*, July, 1950.

Rudikoff, Sonya. "Colette at Eighty," *Partisan Review*, May–June, 1953.

Schmidt, Albert-Marie. "Colette," *Réforme*, August 14, 1954.

Stirling, M. "Colette," *The Atlantic Monthly*, July, 1946.

Thérive, A. "Ecrivains et littérateurs 1900," *Le Crapouillot*, no. 29.

Tortel, Jean. "Colette," *Les Cahiers du Sud*, October, 1954.

Wescott, Glenway. "Introduction," *Short Novels of Colette*. New York, The Dial Press, 1951, pp. vii–lvii.

Willy. "Madame Colette," *L'Action Française*, January 3, 1929.

Willy. "Quelques détails sur la collaboration Colette-Willy," *Les Nouvelles Littéraires*, April 3, 1926.

Index